ALL-IN-ONE IPHONE 15 GUIDE FOR SENIORS

The Step-by-Step Manual to Unlocking
Your Device's Capabilities
with Clear Instructions and Practical Strategies

Brandon Brooks

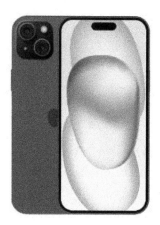

ALL-IN-ONE IPHONE 15 GUIDE FOR SENIORS

Unlock your exclusive BONUSES
tailored just for you!

For our <u>distinguished gentlemen,</u> dive into *'Navigating the golden years,'* your essential guide to mastering retirement with grace and tech-savviness.

And for our <u>inspiring ladies,</u> *'Wellness and connection: a senior woman's companion'* awaits to enrich your journey with health, creativity, and deep connections.

Don't miss out on these valuable resources designed to enhance your golden years.

Simply scan the **QR Code** or follow the link below to access your bonuses.

HTTPS://TINYURL.COM/Y8KEFEWU

Embrace this opportunity to transform your retirement into an <u>era of empowerment and joy.</u>

Download now and <u>start exploring the possibilities that await!</u>

Table of Contents

INTRODUCTION

WELCOME TO IPHONE 15: EMBRACING TECHNOLOGY IN YOUR GOLDEN YEARS

In this digital age, staying connected <u>has never been more crucial,</u> and the iPhone 15 is here to seamlessly integrate technology into the lives of our esteemed seniors.

This innovative device is designed with a user-friendly interface, prioritizing simplicity and accessibility to ensure a smooth transition into the world of modern communication.

With its advanced features, the iPhone 15 caters to the diverse needs of seniors, <u>offering an array of health and wellness apps</u>, intuitive voice commands, and an enhanced display for effortless navigation.

Our mission is **to empower seniors to embrace the advantages of technology**, fostering connectivity with loved ones, accessing valuable information, and enjoying the convenience of digital living.

Join us on this journey as we explore the endless possibilities that the iPhone 15 brings to the golden years, making technology an enriching and enjoyable part of your life.

Embrace the future, stay connected, and <u>unlock the full potential</u> of your golden years with the iPhone 15!

HOW THIS BOOK WILL GUIDE YOU

This guide is here to help seniors understand and make the most of the iPhone 15 without any confusing tech talk. We know technology can be overwhelming, but this guide breaks it down into simple steps.

The iPhone 15 is not just for calls and texts—it can do so much more, like helping you stay connected, organize your tasks, and access important health info.

What makes this guide special is <u>its simplicity</u>. No complicated words or unnecessary details.

We start with the basics, helping you get used to the iPhone's easy-to-use interface.

<u>Each chapter guides you through tasks one step at a time,</u> making sure you understand before moving on.

We cover everything from staying connected through calls, texts, and video chats to exploring useful apps for health, entertainment, finance, and news.

Your security is important too, so we'll show you how to keep your data safe.

And for seniors, **we've got 10 essential tips—simple tricks** to make using your iPhone easier.

Whether you're setting up your iPhone for the first time or wanting to explore more, this guide is a roadmap to help you master it at your own pace.

So, let's start this journey together.

By the end, you won't just be using your iPhone 15, ***you'll be a master at it.***

UNBOXING YOUR NEW COMPANION

UNPACKING AND POWERING ON: YOUR FIRST STEPS WITH THE IPHONE 15.

Unboxing

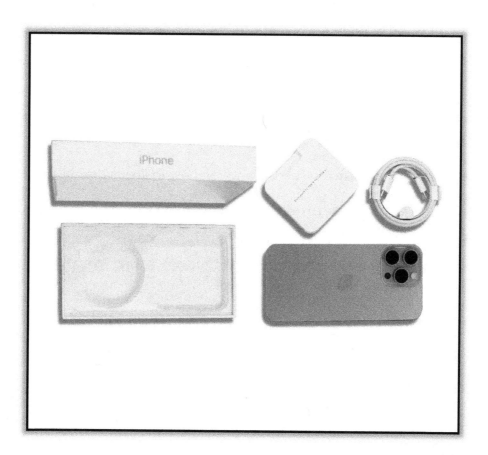

When you open the box of the iPhone 15, it's a really cool moment for people who love tech and even for older folks. Inside the fancy package, there are some interesting things to check out:

Your iPhone 15: This is the main star of the show. Whether you got the regular one, the Plus, or the Pro, each type has its own special features and looks. Older people will like how easy it is to use and all the cool stuff it can do.

USB Type-C to Type-C Cable: Apple changed things up a bit by giving you a special cable. This one is known for being super-fast at moving data around, and it's built to last. Seniors can use it to charge their phone and transfer stuff quickly, and it won't wear out easily.

Documentation and Inserts: There's also some important paperwork in there. You'll get a quick guide to help you start using your new phone, warranty info, and safety instructions. Seniors can read these to get to know their phone better and make sure they can use all its features.

The Iconic Apple Logo Sticker: For people who really like Apple stuff, there's a familiar sticker with the Apple logo in the box. It doesn't do much, but it's a nice touch that makes you feel proud to be an Apple fan.

Remember, the power adapter, AirPods, and Apple Watches are not included. You need to get them separately if you want them.

Initial Setup: Language, Region, and Accessibility Settings

When you take your new iPhone 15 out of the box, there are a few important steps to start using it. First, you need to set up things like language, region, and accessibility. This guide will help you do that, making sure your iPhone 15 is set up just the way you like it from the beginning.

Getting Your Language and Region Right

1. Turn on your iPhone 15 by holding down the side button until you see the Apple logo.

2. You'll see a "Hello" screen. Swipe your finger from left to right to start setting up your phone.+

3. Choose the language you like. Your iPhone 15 has lots of languages, so pick the one that feels just right for you.

4. Now, pick your region. This helps set up things like how dates and times show up, what currency symbols to use, and any special features based on where you are.

BASIC NAVIGATION: UNDERSTANDING THE HOME SCREEN, BUTTONS, AND GESTURES.

The iPhone 15 has buttons that are easy to use, especially for seniors. Let's look at them more closely:

Side Buttons: The iPhone 15 has classic side buttons for volume and power. These buttons are easy to find and press. Seniors can adjust the volume or turn the phone on and off without any trouble.

Action Button (Pro Models): In the iPhone 15 Pro models, there's a special button called the Action Button. It used to be the mute switch, but now it can do different things. Seniors can make it work the way they want, like opening apps quickly or turning on features that help them use the phone better.

USB Type-C Connector (Pro Models): The iPhone 15 Pro models now use a USB Type-C connector instead of the usual one. This change makes it easier to connect the phone to other things. Seniors can use it with more accessories, and it makes transferring pictures and stuff faster.

SIM Card Tray: The tray for the SIM card is in a good spot. It's easy to reach, so seniors can put in or change their SIM cards without any problem. This is useful for those who need to switch SIM cards for different reasons, like when they travel.

PERSONALIZING YOUR DEVICE: ADJUSTING SETTINGS FOR OPTIMAL USE.

Appearance

To customize your display, just go to **Settings**, and then go down to "**Display & Brightness**." You're going to see tons of customizable options.

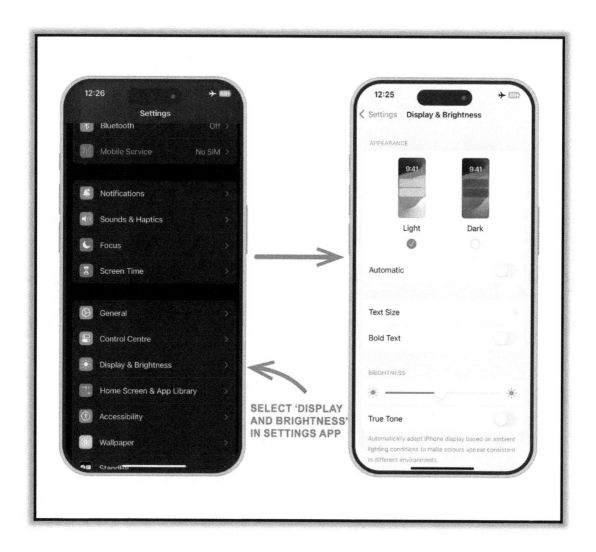

SELECT 'DISPLAY AND BRIGHTNESS' IN SETTINGS APP

First is the "**Appearance**" section. You have the option between "**Light**" and "**Dark**" mode for how your iPhone appears.

By default, your iPhone is in "**Light**," but if we want to make it dark, select "**Dark**" from the Appearance segment, and your iPhone will turn all the background pixels on your phone black while the overlaying text will be white.

TO CHANGE YOUR IPHONE APPEARANCE, TAP THE SELECTOR UNDER PREFFERED MODE

Underneath the "**Light**" and "**Dark**" modes is the "**Automatic**" tab. If you turn this on, it's going to give us a few options to go off of. So, essentially, by turning this on, you can have a scheduled time to change appearance automatically.

So, if you want light mode on from "**Sunset to Sunrise**," it'll stay on during these time periods. As soon as the sun sets, your phone is going to transition into dark mode since it's now nighttime. You can also create your own custom schedule right here.

Text Size

Next is the "**Text Size**" tab. You can change the size of your text. The standard size is fine, but if you want it bigger because you have a hard time seeing the normal-sized text, you can always turn that up. If you want your text on your iPhone to be smaller, you can definitely do that as well.

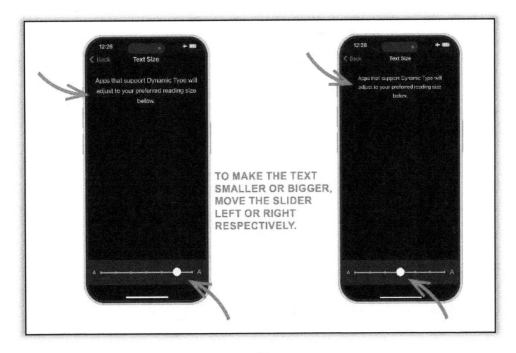

TO MAKE THE TEXT SMALLER OR BIGGER, MOVE THE SLIDER LEFT OR RIGHT RESPECTIVELY.

Bold Text

Next is the "**Bold Text**" toggle. If you turn on the "**Bold Text**" toggle, all the text on your screen is going to turn bold. This is completely up to you.

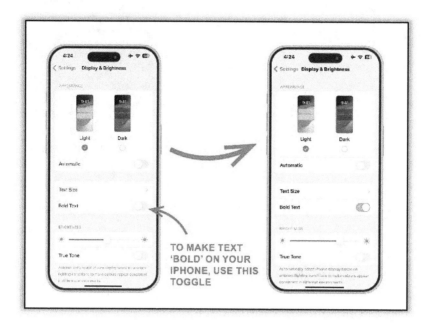

TO MAKE TEXT 'BOLD' ON YOUR IPHONE, USE THIS TOGGLE

Brightness

You can use the "**Brightness**" slider below the "Text Size" tab to manually control your iPhone's brightness. There's also a slider in your iPhone's Control Center for manual brightness control.

True Tone

Below the "Brightness" slider is **True Tone**. True Tone uses a number of sensors to automatically change the color temperature of your iPhone based on the light around you. This makes the display look more natural in different lighting conditions. It is recommended that you turn it on to get the most out of your iPhone's display.

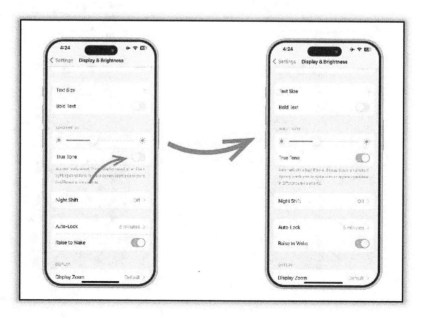

Auto-Lock

Another feature that you might find helpful is Auto-Lock, an iOS feature that determines how long your screen is going to stay unlocked before shutting off. When your iPhone senses that you're staring at the screen, it won't automatically lower the brightness. You can set your auto-lock to activate between 30 seconds and five minutes, or anywhere in between.

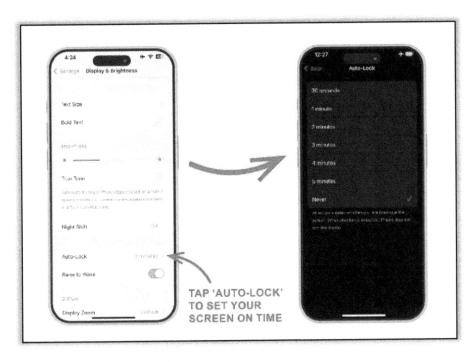

TAP 'AUTO-LOCK' TO SET YOUR SCREEN ON TIME

Always-On Display

Instead of your iPhone screen shutting off, with Always-On Display, the Lock Screen will dial down its brightness but remain viewable, so you can see any updates at any time without having to tap any buttons or touch the device. The screen is just going to be dimmer. And then, when you pick up your iPhone, it starts to get brighter and goes back to its normal display brightness. This is a feature on iPhone 15 Pro models.

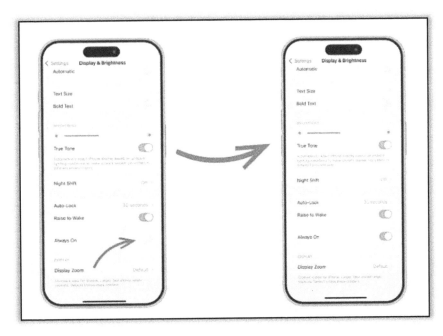

Nevertheless, keep in mind that when it's in your pocket or lying face-down, the screen will go black so that your device can save battery life. This is a great feature for the iPhone 15.

Customize the Lock Screen

Since all iPhone 15 models come preloaded with iOS 17, they also come with a feature that lets you change and edit your Lock Screen without having to go into your iPhone's Settings app.

You can do it right through the Lock Screen, which makes it super convenient and easy. This Lock Screen customization feature offers tons of customizations you can do with these Lock Screens.

Edit the active Lock Screen

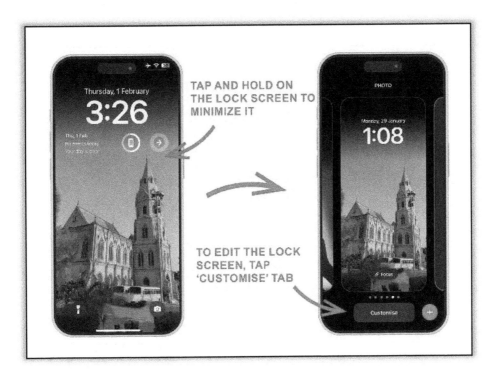

First, if you want to edit the Lock Screen that you currently have, all you have to do is hold down on it, and the screen will minimize, displaying a "**Customize**" button directly below it.

Tap on the button, and the screen will become editable.

Here, you'll be able to change the font type for your date and time, the color, and add certain widgets to your Lock Screen.

To change the color or the font type for your Lock Screen's date and time text, tap on the date or time, and you'll see a box come up with different available fonts and colors to choose from.

You can also swipe the solid color options at the bottom to choose different colors for that specific font.

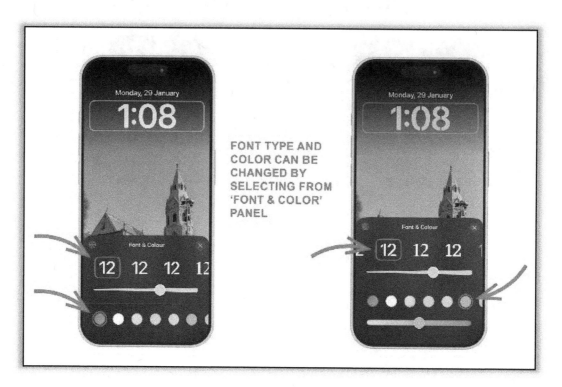

If your preferred color isn't available in the provided options, tap the Eyedropper Tool (shaped like a multicolor sphere) to choose from a color spectrum, color grid, or color slider. With these tools, you can edit your Lock Screen to your taste.

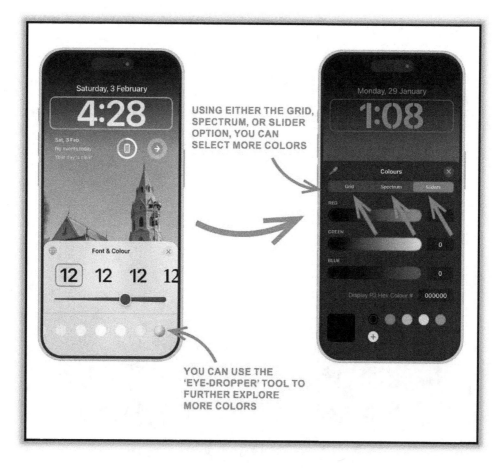

Add Lock Screen widgets

You can also choose what widgets you want to be shown on your Lock Screen. While the Lock Screen is still in **"customize"** mode, tap the **"ADD WIDGETS"** tab right below the time on the Lock Screen, or tap any of the Lock Screen widgets to open the Lock Screen widget library. Here, you'll find all the widgets you can add and remove.

You can also change the color of your Lock Screen while it's still in **"customize"** mode. Simply swipe on the current Lock Screen to change the color options.

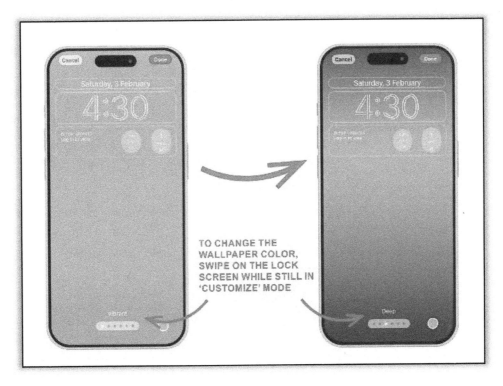

When you're finished customizing the page and you tap **"Done"** at the top-right corner of your iPhone's display, a pop-up box will come up.

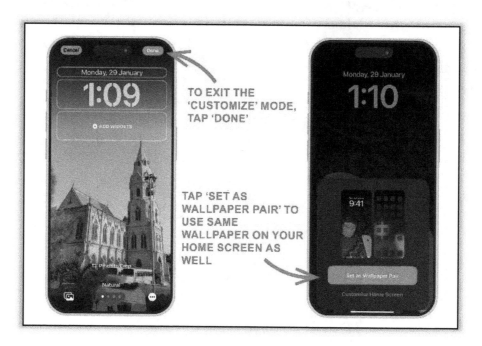

The first option in the pop-up box is **"Set as Wallpaper Pair,"** asking you if you want to set this current Lock Screen wallpaper as your Home Screen wallpaper as well. The **"Customize Home Screen"** option just below the **"Set as Wallpaper Pair"** option lets you customize the Home Screen wallpaper that will be linked to that Lock Screen wallpaper separately.

Create a New Lock Screen

If you want to create a new Lock Screen or switch between Lock Screens, all you have to do is hold down your current Lock Screen until it minimizes. Then swipe left until you reach the **"ADD NEW"** page. Then tap the plus (+) button to open the wallpaper gallery.

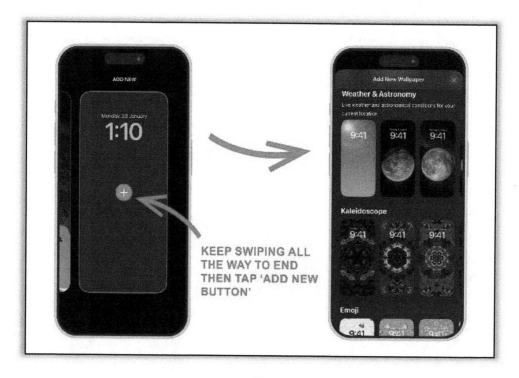

When the wallpaper gallery opens up, you'll find several wallpaper options to choose from. There are tons of wallpapers to choose from: **Photo Shuffle**, **Emoji**, **Featured**, **Collections**, etc.

Add Emoji Wallpapers

One of the most aesthetically pleasing wallpaper options is the "**Emoji**" option. On iOS 17, you can have emojis as the background of your Lock Screen.

If you scroll down to the "**Emoji**" category, you'll find a few that Apple recommends.

But, <u>if you want to create your own,</u> you just scroll back up to the top and tap "**Emoji**" from the provided options. With this, you can select any emoji and make it your Lock Screen.

ACCESSIBILITY FEATURES: MAKING YOUR IPHONE WORK FOR YOU.

Now, let's delve into configuring accessibility settings, which are designed to make your iPhone 15 user-friendly and accessible to everyone, including seniors and individuals with specific needs.

1. To access accessibility settings, go to the **"Settings"** app on your iPhone's home screen. It's represented by an icon that looks like a gear or cogwheel.

2. Scroll down and tap **"Accessibility."** Here, you'll find a wide range of options to customize your iPhone to your liking.

3. Under **"Vision,"** you can adjust settings for Display & Text Size, VoiceOver, Magnifier, and more to cater to your visual needs.

4. In the **"Hearing"** section, you can configure settings related to Sound Recognition, Sound & Haptics, and other audio preferences.

5. **"Touch"** settings allow you to customize features like AssistiveTouch, Touch Accommodations, and more to make the touchscreen easier to use.

6. For those with motor and cognitive challenges, explore options in the **"Motor"** and **"Cognitive"** sections to adapt your iPhone's controls and interactions accordingly.

7. Lastly, don't forget to explore **"Accessibility Shortcut"** for a quick way to enable and toggle accessibility features using a triple-click of the side or home button.

By customizing your accessibility settings, you'll ensure that your iPhone 15 is perfectly tailored to your individual needs, making it a more comfortable and enjoyable device to use.

Once you've configured your preferred language, region, and accessibility settings, you'll be well on your way to personalizing your iPhone 15 to suit your specific requirements.

MAKING COMMUNICATION EFFORTLESS

STAYING CONNECTED: MAKING CALLS, TEXTING, AND USING FACETIME.

MAKING CALLS

The process of making calls on the iPhone 15 is designed to be intuitive & user-friendly. Follow these simple steps for a seamless calling experience:

1. **Check Your Network Connection:** Ensure a stable cellular network connection before initiating a call.

2. **Locate the Phone App:** Find the Phone app on your home screen, recognized by an icon resembling an old-fashioned telephone receiver.

3. **Open the App:** Tap the Phone app icon to open it. This action will direct you to the dial pad.

4. **Dial or Select a Contact:** Manually enter the phone number using the keypad on the dial pad. Alternatively, tap the contacts tab at the bottom of the screen to choose a contact from your saved list.

5. **Use Siri's Voice Command (Optional):** Hold down the home button or say "Hey Siri" to utilize Siri's voice command feature for hands-free calling.

6. **Initiate the Call:** Once you've entered or selected the desired number, press the green call button to start dialing.

7. **Adjust Settings During a Call:** Modify settings like speakerphone, mute, or add another caller via conference calls during active conversations. Access these options through icons prominently displayed on your screen.

8. **End the Call:** To end a call, press the red phone icon. This step is essential to prevent accidental calls or when the conversation concludes, and further communication is unnecessary.

By following these steps, you can make calls effortlessly and take advantage of various features offered by the iPhone 15 during active conversations.

TEXTING

The iPhone 15 provides a seamless and user-friendly platform for efficient texting. Follow these steps for a smooth communication experience:

1. **Unlock Your Device:** Use Face ID or Touch ID to unlock your iPhone.

2. **Open Messages App:** Locate the Messages app on your home screen (green speech bubble icon). Tap to open the application.

3. **Compose a New Message:** Once inside, select the "+" sign to compose a new message.

4. **Add Recipient:** Manually type in the recipient's phone number or choose a contact from your list.

5. **Enter Your Message:** Enter your desired message in the text box provided.

6. **Send Your Message:** Tap on the blue arrow to send your message.

7. **Enhance Your Texting Experience:** Use predictive text by swiping along the letters of each word. Take advantage of Siri's dictation capabilities by tapping on the microphone symbol next to the text field.

8. **Customize Your Messages:** Add a personal touch with emojis or GIFs from the vast collection within the app.

With these straightforward steps, the iPhone 15's texting functionality puts effortless communication at your fingertips.

Setting Up and Using FaceTime

FaceTime is a fantastic way to stay connected with loved ones through video calls. It offers a personal touch by allowing you to see and hear the people you care about, even when they're far away. Here's how to set up and use FaceTime:

Enabling FaceTime:

To enable FaceTime, go to "Settings" > "FaceTime" and toggle the switch to turn it on. You'll also need an Apple ID to use FaceTime.

Making a FaceTime Call:

Open the FaceTime app or go to your Contacts, select a contact, and tap the FaceTime icon to initiate a call. You can also start a FaceTime call during a phone call by tapping FaceTime icon on the call screen.

Group FaceTime:

FaceTime allows group calls with multiple participants. To start a group call, tap the "+" icon in the FaceTime app and add the contacts you want to include.

FaceTime Audio:

You can use FaceTime for audio-only calls. It's a useful feature when you don't want to use video or have limited data connectivity.

FaceTime Effects:

Make your FaceTime calls more fun by using effects like Animoji and Memojis. These animated characters mimic your expressions and add a playful touch to your calls.

FaceTime for Accessibility:

FaceTime includes accessibility features like VoiceOver and closed captions, making it user-friendly for those with hearing or vision impairments.

FaceTime has become a cornerstone of modern communication, enabling users to engage in real-time video conversations with family and friends, bridging geographical distances, and providing a sense of connection and presence that text or voice calls alone cannot achieve. Whether you're catching up with a grandchild's latest adventure or sharing a virtual cup of tea with a dear friend, FaceTime is a valuable tool in your iPhone's communication arsenal.

MANAGING YOUR CONTACTS: ADDING, EDITING, AND ORGANIZING.

Add a New Contact

1. Open the Contact app & press $+$.

2. Then enter the appropriate information in the right fields.

Siri periodically sends you suggestions of new contacts based on your use of other apps. To disable this feature, use the steps below:

1. In Settings app on your iPhone , click **Contacts.**

2. Select **Siri & Search,** & then switch off the **Show Siri Suggestions for Contacts** button.

Share a Contact

1. Click the contact, select **Share Contact,** & choose a sharing method.

Search for a Contact

1. Touch the search field in the contact lists.

2. Then enter the name, phone number, address, or other identifiers for the contact.

Quickly Reach a Contact

You can start a phone call, compose an email, start a text message, or send money with Apple Pay right on the Contacts app.

1. Click the contact & then select an option underneath the contact's name

2. If the contact has multiple phone numbers saved under their name, you can change the default phone number by touching & holding the default tab & choosing a different phone number.

FOR PHONE CALLS AND SMS/MMS MESSAGES, SET PREFFERED LINE

CALL, SEND A MESSAGE, FACETIME, MAIL, OR PAY

Edit a Contact's Information on iPhone

You can add a photo to a contact & add their birthday & other information.

1. Click the contact & tap **Edit** at the top of your screen.

2. Select **Add Photo** to use their photo with the contact.

3. Click the label to change it.

4. Tap ⊕ on an item to add a related name, birthday, social profile, & more.

5. To allow a contact to reach you at any time, even when Do Not Disturb is enabled, click **Ringtone or Text Tone,** then switch on **Emergency Bypass.**

6. Tap ⊖ on an item to remove that information.

7. Once you are satisfied with the changes, click **Done.**

Delete a Contact

1. Click the contact & tap **Edit** at the top of your screen.

2. Then scroll down & select **Delete Contact.**

Change How Contacts are Displayed

Change the arrangement & display of contacts on your iPhone 15

1. In Settings app on your iPhone ⚙, click **Contacts.**

2. Then make your changes.

Hide Duplicate Contacts

If you have multiple entries for one person in Contacts, the best option would be to link all the contact cards so that each contact details appear once. Ideally, the iPhone 15 should automatically link the contacts, but you can use the steps below to manually merge the contacts & remove the duplicates:

1. Click one of the contacts, click **Edit,** & then click **Link Contacts.**

2. Now click the second entry for the same contact & select **Link.**

3. If the names on the multiple entries are different, the iPhone 15 will choose one of the names to use on the unified card. To change the name, click any of the linked cards, click the name of the contact & then select **Use This Name for Unified Card.**

Save the Number you Just Dialed

To save a contact from the phone app,

1. Click **Keypad** in the Phone app 📞, enter a number, & press **Add Number.**

2. Then choose an option: **Add to Existing Contact** (if you have the name stored already) or **Create New Contact** (to save the contact for the first time)

Add a Recent Caller to Contacts

1. Click **Recents** in the Phone app 📞, & press ⓘ beside a number.

Then choose an option: **Add to Existing Contact** (if you have the name stored already) or **Create New Contact** (to save the contact for the first time)

MASTERING VOICEMAIL: NEVER MISS A MESSAGE.

Set Up Voicemail

People drop us voicemails when we miss their calls. Note that you must have set up voicemail before people can drop voicemails for you. To set up,

1. Open the Phone app, press **Voicemail,** & select **Set Up Now**.

2. Enter your preferred voicemail password.

3. Choose a greeting message for your callers using either the **Default** message or creating a **Custom** message; if you select Custom, you will get a prompt to record a new greeting.

Access Your Voicemail Messages

1. Open the Phone app & press **Voicemail.**

2. Tap ▶ to hear the message, ⬆ to share, or 🗑 to delete the message.

3. To recover a message you deleted, press **Deleted Messages,** select the message, & press **Undelete.**

Note that some carriers may permanently erase your deleted messages.

Change Voicemail Password

1. In Settings app on your iPhone ⚙, click **Phone.**

2. Click **Change Voicemail Password** & type in the new password.

Change Voicemail Greeting

1. To use a new greeting, press **Voicemail,** & select **Greeting.**

Setting Up Email

1. Open "Settings" app on your iPhone then scroll down to find "Mail." Tap on it.

2. Select "Accounts," then "Add Account."

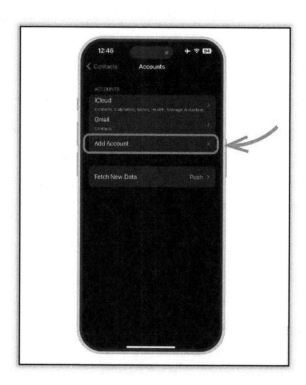

3. Choose your email provider (e.g., iCloud, Gmail, Yahoo, or others) and follow the on-screen instructions to add your email account.

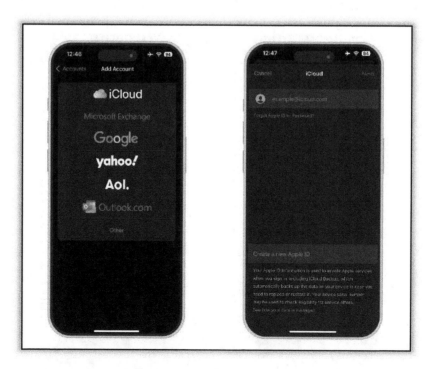

Read an Email

Open your inbox & click on an email to read it.

Print a Picture or Attachment

Click the attachment, click **Share** ⬆ & select **Print.**

Print an Email

Open the email, press ↰ & select **Print.**

Show a Longer Email Preview

The Mail app will show two lines of text for every email you receive. See how to choose up to five preview lines.

1. In Settings app on your iPhone ⚙, click **Mail.**

2. Click **Preview** & choose an option.

Show the Whole Conversation

See all conversations in a single mail thread. To turn on,

1. In Settings app on your iPhone ⚙, click **Mail.**

2. Then switch on **Organize by Thread**

Automatically Send a Copy to Yourself

Receive a copy of every email you send out.

1. In Settings app on your iPhone ⚙, click **Mail.**

2. Then switch on **Always Bcc Myself** under **Composing.** Now you will see the email in your sent folder & your inbox.

Customize Your Email Signature

Add your signature to the mail app to use for outgoing mails.

1. In Settings app on your iPhone ⚙, click **Mail.**

2. Press **Signature** under **Composing** section & touch the text field.

3. Then edit your signature as you like.

4. If you have multiple email accounts on the Mail app, press **Per Account** to create a signature for each account.

Send New Email or Reply to an Email

1. Press ☑ in the Mail app to start a new email.

To reply to an email, open the email, press ↶, & then press **Reply.**

1. If you have multiple email accounts, press the **From** field to choose a different email account.

2. Tap the **To** field & enter the recipients. Tap CC/BCC to copy/ blind copy other recipients.

3. Type your message in the body field. To change formatting as you type, press ‹ above your keyboard & then press Aa.

4. To attach a document, press ‹ above your keyboard & then press ⬜. This will open the Files app, find the document, & click it to attach it to the email.

5. To attach a saved video or photo, press ‹ above your keyboard & then press 🖼️. This will open the Photos app; choose the item you want to attach.

6. To take a new video/ photo & insert it to the email, press ‹, then press 📷 & take your new video or photo. Once done, press **Use Video** or **Use Photo** to include it in your email or press **Retake** to redo the shoot.

7. To scan a document with your camera & attach it to the email, press ‹ & press 🗒️. Position the document on the camera screen, then press any of the volume buttons or tap ◯ to scan the document. Scan as many pages as you have, & press **Save** to finish.

To make changes to the scanned document, click it & do any of the below:

1. Press ⌗ to crop the photo

2. Press ● to apply a filter

3. Press ↰ to rotate

4. Press 🗑 to delete the scanned document.

Show To & CC Labels in your Inbox

Turn on the To & CC labels in your messages.

1. In Settings app on your iPhone ◉ , click **Mail.**

2. Then switch on **Show To/Cc Labels** under **Message List.**

Download Email Attachments

When you receive an email with an attachment, follow the steps below to download the attachment:

1. Open the email with the attachment, touch & hold the attachment & select "**Save to Files**" or "**Save Image.**"

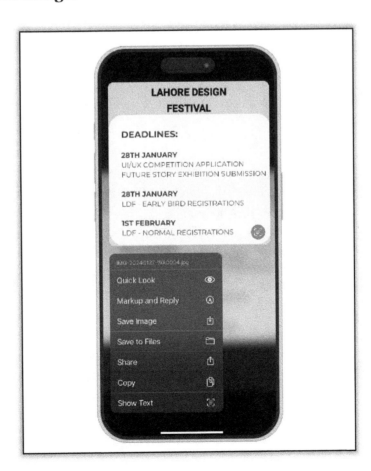

2. Images will be saved in Photos app & documents will be saved in the Files app.

Mark Addresses Outside Certain Domains

Get a warning sign whenever you receive emails from or send emails to domains outside your organization. To enter the allowed domains,

1. In Settings app on your iPhone ⚙, click **Mail.**

2. Scroll to **Composing** & select **Mark Addresses.**

3. Then enter your organization domains like apple.com. Separate multiple domains with commas.

Organize your Mailboxes

Create new mailboxes, reorder or delete existing ones, & more.

Open the Mail app & press ‹ in the top left part of your screen, press **Edit,** & organize the website using any of the steps below:

a. To reorder the mailboxes, hold the ≡ icon next to a mailbox until you see it lift up, then pull it to a new position.

b. Tick the checkboxes beside a mailbox to add it to the mailbox list.

c. To create a new mailbox, press **New Mailbox** at the bottom right part of your screen.

d. To change a mailbox name, press the mailbox, click the current title, clear the name, & enter a new name.

e. To delete a mailbox, press the mailbox & select **Delete Mailbox.**

Use Mail Privacy Protection

Prevent others from knowing when you read their emails as well as accessing other information about your Mail activity including accessing your location from your sent emails. Note that you need to subscribe to iCloud+ to enjoy this service.

1. In Settings app on your iPhone ⚙, click **Mail.**

2. Click the "**Privacy Protection**" option & switch on the **Protect Mail Activity** button.

Hide My Email on iPhone

Apple assigns you a random email address that you can use to send & receive emails. This random address is tied to your original address so that you can access all correspondence in the original email without revealing your real identity.

To send an email using this format,

1. Press ✑ in the Mail app to start a new email.

To reply to an email, open the email, press ↰, & then press **Reply.**

1. Enter the recipient & the subject of the email. You can only have one recipient to use this feature.

2. Press the '**From**' button, press it again & click **Hide My Email.** You will find a new email address in the From field.

3. When you have a response to your email, the response will be forwarded to your original email address.

Manage Hide My Email Addresses

Generate your own new & random email addresses, change the forwarding address, & lots more.

1. In Settings app on your iPhone ⚙, click **your name.**

2. Select **iCloud** & click **Hide My Email.**

3. To create a new 'Hide My Email' address, click **Create New Address.**

4. To delete any 'Hide My Email' address, click the address under **Create New Address,** & click **Deactivate Email Address.** This email address will no longer forward received emails to you.

5. To change your real email address that receives the forwarded messages, click **Forward To** & select a different email address. The email addresses must be available with your Apple ID.

6. To copy the 'Hide My Email' address, click the address, press & hold the 'Hide My Email' section, then press **Copy** & paste in the desired app.

Flag an Email

Flag an email that you want to attend to at a later time.

1. Open the email, press ↰, & then select **Flag.**

2. Click the colored dot to select a color for the flag. You can use the colors to set priority for the flagged emails.

3. Press ⚑ to remove the flag or change the color.

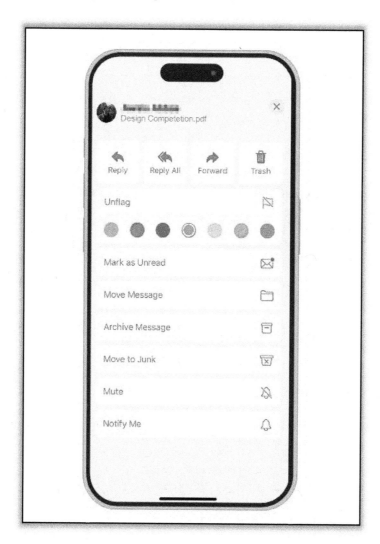

Block Specific Senders

When you receive an email from an address you want to block,

1. Open the email, click their email address, & press **Block this Contact**

Delete Emails

You can delete emails in any of the ways below:

1. Open the email & press 🗑 at the end of the email.

2. Open the mail app, scroll through the mail list, & swipe left on an email, then select **Trash** from the options. Or swipe an email all the way to the left to automatically delete it.

3. To delete more than one email, open the mail app, click **Edit,** click all the emails, & press **Trash.**

Recover Deleted Emails

1. Open the Mail app & press ‹ in the top left part of your screen.

2. Click on the Trash mailbox & press the email you wish to recover.

3. Press ↰, select **Move Message,** & select the inbox mailbox or other mailbox of choice.

Disable Email Deletion Confirmation

When you want to delete an email, you will receive a prompt to confirm your action. To turn off this prompt,

1. In Settings app on your iPhone ⚙, click **Mail.**

2. Scroll to **Messages** & disable **Ask Before Deleting.**

Archive Instead of Delete

You can choose to archive emails rather than delete them.

1. In Settings app on your iPhone ⚙, click **Mail.**

2. Click **Accounts,** click your email provider, & select your email account.

3. Press **Advanced** & select the Archive mailbox for storing discarded emails.

With this option turned off, follow the steps below to delete an email:

1. Find the email, press & hold 🗄 & then click **Trash Message.**

Choose How Long to Keep Deleted Emails

Keep deleted emails up to the maximum time allowed by your email provider.

1. In Settings app on your iPhone ⊚ , click **Mail.**

2. Click **Accounts,** click your email provider, & select your email account.

3. Press **Advanced,** click **Remove,** & choose a time interval.

Mark an Email as Junk

Move an email to your spam or junk folder.

1. Open the email, click ↜ & select **Move to Junk.**

Change Mail Notification Settings

1. In Settings app on your iPhone ⊚ , click **Mail.**

2. Click **Notification** & switch on **Allow Notification.**

3. Click **Customize Notifications** & click the email account you want to change.

4. Then customize as you like.

Mute Email Notifications

Mute notifications from a busy email thread. This will not mute notifications for all emails.

1. Open the email, click ↜ & select **Mute.**

Receive Notification of Replies to an Email or Thread

Get notified when you receive emails from a thread or sender.

1. Open an email, click ↜ & select **Notify Me.**

2. When drafting an email, click the subject field, press 🔔& select **Notify Me.**

EXPLORING THE WORLD OF APPS AND INTERNET

APP ESSENTIALS: DOWNLOADING AND USING KEY APPS.

The App Store is your one-stop destination for discovering, downloading, and updating apps on your iPhone 15. It's a virtual marketplace filled with a vast selection of apps that cater to an array of interests and needs. Whether you're seeking productivity tools, entertainment, or utilities, the App Store has you covered. Here's an overview of how to navigate the App Store:

1. **Accessing the App Store:** To access App Store, just tap the "App Store" icon on your home screen. The icon is easily identifiable with a blue background and a white letter "A."

2. **Home Page:** The App Store's home page showcases featured apps, curated collections, and trending categories. It's an excellent place to discover new and popular apps.

3. **Search:** Utilize search bar located at the bottom of your screen to locate specific apps. You can search by app name, category, or relevant keywords.

4. **Categories:** Tap "Categories" to explore apps organized into various categories such as "Games," "Health & Fitness," "Education," and many more.

5. **Today:** The "Today" tab provides app recommendations, reviews, and articles highlighting noteworthy apps and games.

6. **Updates:** Under the "Updates" tab, you can view & install available updates for your installed apps.

7. **Account:** Your Apple ID profile icon is located in the upper right corner. Here, you can access your account settings, purchased apps, and more.

8. **App Details:** When you select an app, you'll see its details page, featuring an app description, screenshots, user reviews, and ratings. You can also tap the "Get" button to download free apps or the price button for paid apps.

9. **Install and Updates:** To install an app, tap the "Get" or price button. If it's a paid app, you'll need to confirm the purchase with your Apple ID password or Face ID/Touch ID. To update apps, navigate to the "Updates" tab, and tap "Update" next to the app's name.

10. **Wish List:** You can add apps to your Wish List for future consideration. To do so, tap the Share icon on an app's details page and select "Add to Wish List."

11. **Redeem Gift Cards and Promo Codes:** If you have App Store gift cards or promo codes, you can redeem them by scrolling to the bottom of the "Today" tab and selecting "Redeem Gift Card or Code."

12. **In-App Purchases and Subscriptions:** Be aware that some apps offer in-app purchases and subscriptions. You can manage these under "Settings" > "iTunes & App Store" > "Subscriptions."

Downloading and Organizing Apps

Downloading Apps:

1. **Access the App Store:** Tap the "App Store" icon on your home screen to open it.

2. **Search for Apps:** Use the search bar at the bottom to find the app you want. You can search by app name, category, or keywords.

3. **App Details:** Tap on the app's icon to view its details, including a description, screenshots, user reviews, and ratings.

4. **Download the App:** If the app is free, tap the "Get" button to start download. If it's a paid app, tap the price button & confirm the purchase with your Apple ID password or Face ID/Touch ID.

5. **Wait for Download:** App will begin downloading, and you'll spot its icon on your home screen. You can keep an eye on the download's progress through the app's icon.

Organizing Apps:

1. **Home Screen:** Your home screen is where you will locate the applications that you use the most regularly. Organizing them can be accomplished by holding down one app icon until all of the icons begin to wiggle on their own.

2. **Rearrange Icons:** While the icons are wiggling, drag an app icon to a new location on the home screen. You can also create app folders by dragging one app icon onto another. Give the folder a name and add more apps to it.

3. **Delete Apps:** To delete an app, tap the "x" icon in the corner of the app's icon while the icons are wiggling. Deleting an app will remove it from your device but not your App Store purchase history.

4. **App Library:** Swipe left to access your App Library, where apps are automatically categorized into groups like "Recently Added," "Social," and "Entertainment." You can search for apps using search bar at the top or browse through categories.

5. **Search for Apps:** To find a specific app, swipe down on the home screen or App Library to reveal the search bar. Type the app's name, and the search results will appear.

6. **Organize in Folders:** You can create folders in the App Library by dragging one app icon onto another. This is an excellent way to keep your apps organized without cluttering your home screen.

7. **Offload Unused Apps:** To save storage space, you can enable the "Offload Unused Apps" feature in "Settings" > "App Store." This will automatically remove apps that you rarely use but keep their data, allowing you to reinstall them when needed.

BROWSING MADE EASY: USING SAFARI FOR INTERNET ACCESS.

Safari is to Apple what Chrome is to Google. This section shows you different tips for operating & customizing the Safari app 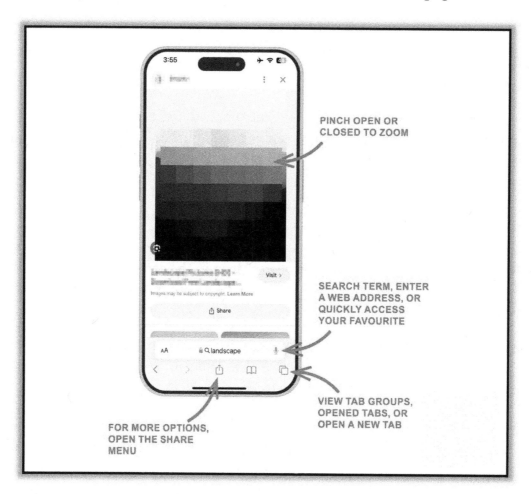.

Surf the Web on Safari

1. Open the Safari app from the app library or home screen.

2. Enter web address in the address field or enter a search phrase to get options.

3. Double press the top edge of your screen to return to the top of the app screen from any part of the page.

4. Pull down from the topmost edge of the page to refresh the page.

5. Rotate your iPhone 15 to landscape to view more content on the page.

PINCH OPEN OR CLOSED TO ZOOM

SEARCH TERM, ENTER A WEB ADDRESS, OR QUICKLY ACCESS YOUR FAVOURITE

VIEW TAB GROUPS, OPENED TABS, OR OPEN A NEW TAB

FOR MORE OPTIONS, OPEN THE SHARE MENU

6. Press at the end of a webpage to share the web link.

7. Press & hold a link in Safari for a preview of the web page without launching the page.

8. Click the preview or select **Open** to go to the web page.

TAP AND HOLD A LINK TO SEE THE URL AND THESE OPTIONS

9. To remain on the current page & exit the preview, touch anywhere outside the preview space.

Add Safari to Your Home Screen

If you can't find the Safari app on your home screen but want it there, use the steps below to add it back:

1. Go to the App Library & search for 'Safari' in the search field or swipe to the app.

2. Then touch & hold the app icon & press **Add to Home Screen.**

Search the Web

In Safari, you can use the search field to go directly to a website by inputting the website URL or entering a search term to find the information across multiple websites.

1. Open the Safari app & click the search space.

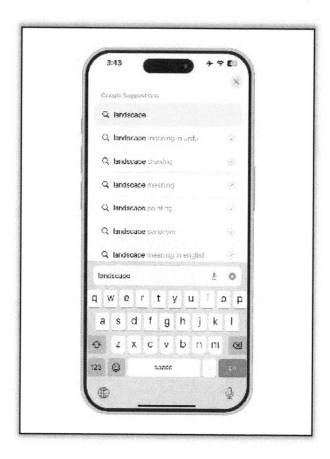

2. Type the URL in the search space or enter a search phrase.

3. If searching using a phrase, click a suggestion to go to it or click **Go** on your keyboard to search specifically for the term you entered.

Select Default Search Engine

1. In Settings app on your iPhone ⊙, click **Safari.**

2. Click **Search Engine** & make your choice.

Translate a Webpage

Use Safari to get the translated version of a page.

1. Click ᴬA on the webpage, then click 🗛.

2. Note that not all languages are available for this service.

Change Screen Layout in Safari

You can change the screen layout to another type. Your selection will determine the location of the search bar – the Tab Bar layout keeps search bar at the bottom of your screen, while the Single Tap layout keeps the bar at the top. Choose a layout with the steps below:

1. Scroll to the left side of the search field & press ᴬA.

2. Then select an option: '**Show Bottom Tab Bar**' or '**Show Top Address Bar.**'

3. In Settings app on your iPhone , click **Safari.**

4. Swipe to **Tabs** & select an option: '**Single Tab**' or '**Tab Bar.**'

Customize Your Start Page

Customize the Safari start page to have new background images & other options.

1. Open a new tab, press ⬜, & then press ＋.

2. Swipe to the end of the app screen & press **Edit.**

3. Now you can customize/ turn on options for your Safari start page:

   Favorites – find a shortcut to websites you marked as favorites on the start page.
   Siri Suggestions – turn this on so that Siri can suggest webpages as you search.
   Shared with You – to view links that people shared with you in Mail, Messages, & other apps.
   Frequently Visited – see the list of your frequently visited websites here.
   Privacy Report – for a report of the number of websites & trackers that Safari blocked from tracking your web activity.
   Reading List – see a list of pages in your Reading List.
   iCloud Tabs – to see other open tabs from all your other Apple devices that are linked to the same Apple ID as your iPhone 15.

Note that changes to the start page settings will apply to all your linked Apple devices using the same Apple ID.

Change Text Size

Increase or decrease the size of text on a website.

1. Scroll to the left side of the search field & press AA.

2. Use the small A to reduce the text size & the big A to increase it.

Open a Link in a New Tab

When you come across links on a webpage, you can choose to open them on a new tab.

1. Press & hold the new link, then select **Open in New Tab.**

When you open a link in a new tab, the iPhone will automatically take you to the new screen. However, you can change the setting to remain on the current tab:

1. In Settings app on your iPhone ◎, click **Safari.**

2. Click **Open Links** & then click **In Background.**

Search Within Websites

You can search for a term within a website. For example, you can enter "crypto amazon" to go straight to all crypto-related results on Amazon. Use the steps below to turn this setting on:

1. In Settings app on your iPhone ◎, click **Safari.**

2. Then switch on **Quick Website Search.**

Search the Page

To find a specific phrase or words on a webpage,

1. Click ⬆& select **Find on Page.**

2. Type the phrase or words in the search box & press ∨ to jump to the different mentions of that word.

Browse Open Tabs

See all open tabs on one page and navigate through them.

1. Click ⬜in the Safari app & click ⊗in the top right side of the preview to close a tab.

2. To open a tab, click it or click **Done** to return to the single tab.

Reopen Recently Closed Tabs

1. Click ⬜in the Safari app, press ＋& click any of the recently closed tabs.

See Your Favorite Websites in Search or New Tabs

This setting will allow you to see your favorite websites when you click the search field or open a new tab. To turn on,

1. In Settings app on your iPhone ⚙, click **Safari.**

2. Click **Favorites** & select the folder that should show in the categories above.

View All Open Tabs Across your Other Devices

All devices must be signed in to iCloud using the same Apple ID.

1. In Settings app on your iPhone ⚙, click your name.

2. Click **iCloud** & switch on **Safari.**

3. Click ⬚ in the Safari app, press +, & then swipe to see all the open tabs.

4. To delete a tab from the list, press & hold that link & then select **Choose.** The link will be removed from your iPhone 15 but not from the original device.

Organize Your Tabs

You can use a Tab group to organize your tabs & make it easy to return to them later.

1. Click ⬚ in the Safari app to see your open tabs.

2. Press & hold one tab & select **Move to Tab Group.**

3. Click **New Tab Group** & title the group.

4. Click ⌄ in the lower section of your screen to move between Tab Groups.

Move a Tab to Another Group

1. Click ⧉ in the Safari app to see your open tabs.

2. Press & hold one tab to move it. When you see a menu option, click **Move to Tab Group.**

3. Select an existing group or create a new one.

Close All Open Tabs

1. Press & hold the ⧉ icon on a page, then click **Close All Tabs.**

Add Pages to Bookmark

Bookmarks are perfect for pages you want to save and read later/

1. Open the webpage, click ⬆ & select **Add Bookmark.**

View & Organize Your Bookmarks

1. Click 📖 in Safari to view your bookmarks.

2. To organize, click **Edit** & click an option on your screen:

   Create a new folder
   Rename bookmarks
   Delete bookmarks
   Reorder bookmarks

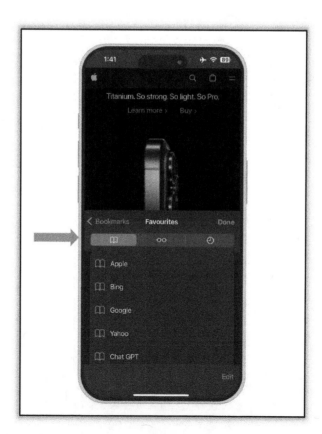

Create Your Favorites Lists

1. Open the webpage, click ⬆️ & select **Add to Favorites.**

Edit Your Favorites Lists

1. Click 📖in Safari & click **Favorites.**

2. Then click **Edit** to rename, delete, or rearrange your favorites.

Add Pages to/ View your Reading List

Just like bookmarks, add pages you want to read later to your reading list. To add the current webpage,

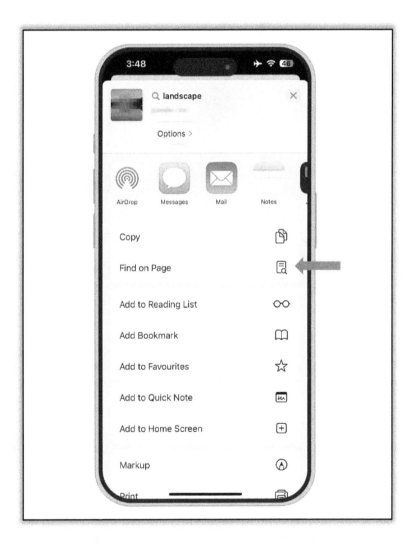

1. Click 📖in Safari & select Add to Reading List.

2. To view the list, press 📖 & then press ◯◯ .

3. Swipe a list to the left to delete it from the reading list.

Show Readers

Reader blocks all ads and navigation menus on a webpage

1. Press ^{A}A & click **Show Reader.**

2. Press ^{A}A & click **Hide Reader** to return to the full page.

Show Reader isn't available on a website if the option is dimmed.

Save a Webpage as a PDF

Before you save a webpage, you can write & draw notes, highlight your favorite parts, & make other edits.

1. Press ⬆️ on the webpage to begin saving.

2. To write & make a selection on the webpage, press **Markup** Ⓐ, select your tool & make your changes.

3. Press **Done** & continue with the onscreen instructions.

Automatically Use Reader for a Website

Customize a website to always use Reader (block ads & distraction menus).

1. Press ^{A}A on a supported website & click **Website Settings.**

2. Then switch on **Use Reader Automatically**

You can also turn this setting for all supported websites.

1. In Settings app on your iPhone ⚙, click **Safari.**Click **Reader** & switch on the menu.

Block Pop-Ups

1. In Settings app on your iPhone ⚙, click **Safari.**

2. Then switch on **Block Pop-ups.**

View Privacy Report

This gives a report of the number of websites & trackers that Safari blocked from tracking your web activity. To get the report,

1. Press ^{A}A & select 🛡**Privacy Report**.

Use Private Browsing Mode

By using the private browsing mode, you are able to browse without leaving a history behind. That is, your activities aren't tracked & won't appear on your history.

1. Open Safari & click ⧉.

2. Click ⌄ in the bottom of your screen (in the center of the Tab bar), then select **Private.**

To exit private browsing mode,

1. Click ⧉ & press ⌄ to see the different Tab Group, click on a group outside the Private Group to exit this mode.

Clear Cache in Safari

By clearing the cache, you are deleting website history & recent searches from your iPhone 15

1. In Settings app on your iPhone ⚙, click **Safari.**

2. Then select '**Clear History & Website Data.**'

STAYING INFORMED AND ENTERTAINED: POPULAR APPS FOR SENIORS.

There are numerous iPhone apps designed to cater to the needs & preferences of seniors, providing functionalities ranging from health and wellness to social connectivity and entertainment. Here are some popular iPhone apps for seniors:

AARP Now: The official app for AARP offers news, health tips, and discounts for AARP members.

Magnifying Glass with Light: Turns your iPhone into a magnifying glass with a built-in light for reading small text.

MyFitnessPal: A health and fitness app that helps users track nutrition, exercise, and overall wellness.

Lumosity: Cognitive skills, memory, and attention are all areas that can be improved through the use of brain training games.

Words with Friends: A popular word game that allows seniors to play with friends or random opponents.

Zoom or Skype: Video conferencing apps for staying connected with friends and family, especially useful for virtual meetings.

Audible: An audiobook app that lets seniors enjoy books through audio format, perfect for those who prefer listening over reading.

Big Button Calculator: A simple calculator app with large buttons for easy use.

The Weather Channel: Stay updated on local weather forecasts and conditions.

ONLINE SAFETY: PROTECTING YOURSELF ON THE INTERNET.

Ensuring your online safety, particularly on your iPhone, is essential to safeguarding your privacy & maintaining security. Here are some tips for online safety on your iPhone:

1. **Keep Your iPhone Updated:** Frequently update both your iPhone's operating system and apps to ensure you have the most recent security patches.

2. **Enable Two-Factor Authentication (2FA):** Turn on the two-factor authentication feature for your Apple ID today. If you want to gain access to your account, you will need to have a code sent to the device you trust. This provides an additional layer of security.

3. **Use Strong, Unique Passwords:** Employ intricate passwords for your accounts, steering clear of using the same password across various services. Contemplate utilizing a trustworthy password manager to generate and securely store robust, individual passwords.

4. **Enable Face ID or Touch ID:** Use biometric authentication (Face ID or Touch ID) to secure your device and apps. This adds an extra layer of protection and convenience.

5. **Review App Permissions:** Regularly review and manage app permissions in your iPhone settings. Only grant necessary permissions to apps, such as location services, camera, and microphone.

6. **Be Cautious with Email and Messages:** Steer clear of clicking on dubious links or downloading attachments from unfamiliar sources in emails and messages to minimize potential risks. Be wary of phishing attempts and verify the authenticity of messages, especially if they ask for sensitive information.

7. **Use a Virtual Private Network (VPN):** When you are utilizing public Wi-Fi networks, you should think about using a virtual private network (VPN) to encrypt your internet connection. This makes it easier to prevent prospective eavesdroppers from accessing your info.

8. **Secure Wi-Fi Connections:** Connect to secure and trusted Wi-Fi networks. Avoid connecting to public Wi-Fi networks without proper security measures.

9. **Review App Privacy Labels:** Check the privacy labels in the App Store for details on how apps handle your data. This information can help you make informed choices about which apps to install.

10. **Regularly Review and Update Apps:** Delete apps you no longer use and update the ones you keep to ensure you have the latest security features.

11. **Use Safari with Content Blockers:** In Safari settings, enable content blockers to prevent websites from tracking your browsing activity.

12. **Enable Find My iPhone:** Turn on "Find My iPhone" to locate your device if it's lost or stolen. This feature also lets you to remotely erase your data if necessary.

13. **Set Up Emergency SOS:** Familiarize yourself with Emergency SOS features on your iPhone, including how to make an emergency call and share your location with emergency services.

14. **Beware of Scams:** Be cautious of unsolicited calls, messages, or emails claiming to be from reputable sources. Avoid sharing personal information unless you're certain of the legitimacy.

15. **Educate Yourself:** Stay informed about common online threats and scams. Apple's official support resources and security documentation can provide valuable information.

CAPTURING AND CHERISHING MEMORIES

MASTERING THE CAMERA: TAKING AND EDITING PHOTOS AND VIDEOS.

Open Camera

1. Swipe left on the lock screen or click the camera 📷 icon on the home screen to launch camera.

2. A green dot shows at the top right side of your screen to notify you that the camera is in use.

Switch Between Camera Modes

The Photo mode is the default mode when you open the Camera app. However, you will find other modes when you swipe on the app.

1. Swipe right or left to find the following camera modes:

   Video – for video recordings
   Slo-mo – to add a slow-motion effect in your video
   Time-lapse – for capturing series of movement over a period of time.
   Portrait – this mode adds effect to your photos.
   Pano – best for capturing panoramic landscapes or similar scenes.
   Cinematic – this mode adds effect to your videos.
   Square – photos taken in this mode will have a square ratio. To choose a ratio, press ⌃ & select an option.

Take a Selfie

You can take a selfie in Portrait, Photo, and Video modes.

1. Tap 🔄 in a compatible mode to switch to the front-facing camera.

2. Position yourself & then use any of the volume buttons or the ⭕ button to take your photo or record your video.

You can also customize the setting to use the mirrored selfie. This option captures the photo just as if you are staring into the phone. To switch on this option,

1. In Settings app on your iPhone ⚙, click **Camera.**

2. Then switch on **Mirror Front Camera.**

Take Macro Videos & Photos

This setting allows you to take an extreme close-up shot of the subject. The camera lens focuses on the subject to get a very close-up shot. To take macro videos or photos,

1. Open the camera app & go very close to your subject, up to 2 centimeters close, then the camera will instantly & automatically focus on the subject.

Control Macro Videos & Photos

To give you more control over your photos & videos, Apple allows you to manually switch the camera lens from the Wide to the Ultra-wide camera to take your macro content. To turn on,

1. In Settings app on your iPhone ⚙, click **Camera** & then switch on **Macro Control.**

2. Open the camera app & move close to the subject.

3. To block switching to the ultra-wide camera lens, click 🌷 & the camera will remain on the wide camera lens. If the video or image shows up blurry, you may back up or press .5x to switch to the ultra-wide lens.

4. Tap 🌼 to allow the camera automatic switch between the two lens.

Take a Photo

1. Press the ⭕ button on the camera app screen or press one of the volume buttons to take your photo.

2. Pinch open or closed to zoom in or out. Or toggle between 0.5x, 1x, 2x, 2.5x, & 3x to zoom in or out quickly.

3. Or press & hold the zoom controls & use the slider to zoom in or out.

Add Filters to your Photo

Filters give your pictures a color effect. To add,

1. Switch to either Portrait or Photo mode, press ⬆, & then press ⊛.

2. You will find the filters below the viewer; swipe right & left to preview each filter, then click one to use it on your photo.

Turn the Flash on or Off

The iPhone 15 camera is set to automatically turn on flash when shooting in a dark environment. Follow the steps below to manually turn on the flash

1. Press ⚡in the screen to turn flash on or off.

2. Then press ⬆, & press ⚡to choose an option: **Off, On,** or **Auto.**

Set Camera Timer

With timers, the camera app allows some seconds before taking a shot. This allows you enough time to position your iPhone and join in the picture.

1. Press ⬆, tap ⏱, select a time & then press the ◯ button to begin the timer.

2. The camera app will take the shot once the time is up.

Straighten Your Shot

When it seems like your photo isn't straightened, use this setting to straighten your shot.

1. In Settings app on your iPhone ⚙, click **Camera.**

2. Then switch on **Grid** & proceed to set & take your photo.

Adjust Camera Focus & Exposure

When you open the camera app to take a photo, the iPhone 15 will automatically set the lens focus & exposure, & the face detection feature balances the exposure level of all faces in the shot. To manually control this feature,

1. Open the camera app & remain in the Photo mode.

2. Touch your screen to display the exposure setting.

3. Touch the side of the screen you want to move the focus area.

4. Then drag the ☀to adjust the exposure.

You can also lock the exposure settings for future shots. To do this,

1. Press ⌃, tap ⊕, & use the slider to customize the exposure. The settings will apply the next time you open the camera app.

To save the settings so that it doesn't reset,

1. In Settings app on your iPhone ⚙, click **Camera.**

2. Click **Preserve Settings** & switch on **Exposure Adjustment.**

Use Photographic Styles

This setting adds warmth and tone to your photos just like you get when you go into a photo studio. You have four pre-set styles to choose from when using this mode. To choose a style,

1. Tap ⌃ in the camera app, press ▣, & swipe left to see the different styles: Warm, Cool, Vibrant, & Rich Contrast.

To customize any style you choose, press the **Warmth** & **Tone** buttons at the bottom of the screen, then use the slider to adjust the result. Press ↺ to reset the changes.

2. Press ▣ to use the style as you take your photo, & press the ◯ button to take your photo.

3. To adjust or change a style that you choose, press ⬡ at the top part of your screen.

To modify or fine-tune a Photographic Style that you've configured, tap ⬡ at the top of the screen.

Change Photographic Styles in Settings

Use this setting to choose a different photographic style:

1. In Settings app on your iPhone ⚙, click **Camera.**

2. Scroll to **Photo Capture** & select **Photographic Styles.**

3. Use your finger to navigate through the four styles, & then click **Use (Name of Style)** on the style you want.

Take Live Photos

In Live photos, you can play the scene before & after a photo was captured, including the sounds in the background.

1. Click the ◎ icon in the Photo Mode to take a Live Photo; the icon will show at the top of your screen to confirm that the feature is on.

2. Press the ○ button to capture a live photo.

3. To watch the Live Photo, press the photo thumbnail at the lower end of your screen, then press & hold the screen to watch it

4. Press the ◎ button again to turn off a live photo.

Use Burst Mode To Capture Action Shots

Burst mode is the perfect mode for shooting moving subjects. It takes multiple shots of a moving object in quick succession. The feature works with both the front & rear-facing camera. To use,

1. Stay on Photo mode, then swipe the ○ button to the left side of your screen & continue to hold to take quick photos. The counter will display the number of shots you have taken already.

2. Release your finger to stop recording.

3. Then press the Burst thumbnail at the lower end of your screen to see the photos. To choose, press **Select** & tap the photos you want to keep, then press **Done.**

4. To delete the complete burst, press 🗑 in the photo thumbnail.

Another way to take burst shots is to touch & hold the volume up button while the camera app is open. To turn on this setting,

1. In Settings app on your iPhone ◎ , click **Camera.**

2. Then switch on **Use Volume Up for Burst.**

Take Photos in Portrait Mode

This mode adds a special effect to your photos. It keeps the focus on the subject while blurring the background.

1. Swipe to Portrait mode & use the onscreen tips to frame your subject inside the yellow portrait box.

2. Then drag the ⬡ icon to select a lighting effect. Each option will give you a preview of how the photo would look.

3. Once you are satisfied with the preview, press the ◯ button to capture your photo.

You can remove the portrait mode effect from photos you capture on your iPhone 15. To do so,

1. Open the Photo in the Photos app then click **Edit.**

2. Then press **Portrait** to switch the effect off or on.

Adjust Depth Control in Portrait Mode

This setting sets the level of the background blur in photos taken in portrait mode.

1. Properly frame your subject in the Portrait mode.

2. Then press 𝑓 in the upper-right corner of your screen to see the Depth Control slider.

3. Use the slider to change the effect, then press the ◯ button to take your photo.

Adjust Portrait Lighting Effects in Portrait Mode

You can customize the intensity & position of the Portrait lighting effect to brighten & smoothen facial features or sharpen eyes.

1. Drag the ⬡ icon in Portrait mode to select a lighting effect.

2. Press ⬢ above the screen to see the Portrait Lighting slider under the frame.

3. Use the slider to change the effect, then press the ◯ button to take your photo.

Night Mode Photos on your iPhone

Use night mode in low-light situations to brighten your shots & capture more detail.

1. Open the camera app. Night mode will turn on automatically in low-light situations. You will find a yellow button at the top left of your screen with a number in it to tell how many seconds the iPhone 15 will take to shoot.

2. To try out different features with Night mode, press ◉ & use the slider to move between Max & Auto timers. The auto timer determines the time automatically, while Max timers use the longest time.

3. Whatever setting you choose will be used when next you open the camera app.

4. Press the ◯ button & hold your camera still to capture your photo.

5. If the camera detects movement while the screen is recording, crosshairs will appear in the frame.

6. Press the **Stop** button to stop shooting before the timer is done.

Adjust Shutter Volume

1. Use the volume buttons to modify the shutter volume.

2. Or open the camera app, swipe downwards from the right top corner to open the Control Panel, then drag 🔊 to increase or decrease volume.

3. Or use the Ring/Silent button on your iPhone 15 to mute the shutter sound.

Turn off HDR Videos

You can also turn off HDR for your videos.

1. In Settings app on your iPhone ⚙, click **Camera** & switch off the **HDR Video** button.

Turn off Automatic HDR

HDR (High Dynamic Range) adds effect to your photos. The setting takes several pictures and then combines them to give more detail & highlight in the photos. By default, the iPhone would automatically turn on this setting when it thinks its right but you can switch off the auto option and manually operate this setting.

1. In Settings app on your iPhone ⚙, click **Camera** & switch off **Smart HDR.**

2. Return to the camera viewfinder & click **HDR** to switch it on or off.

Record a Video

1. Open the camera app & swipe to **Video** Mode.

2. Then press any of the volume buttons or the Record button on your screen to start recording.

3. While recording, you can pinch closed or open to zoom in & out & tap the white ⭘ button to take a still photo.

4. Press any of the volume buttons or the Record button on your screen to stop recording.

The iPhone 15 camera records video at 30 frames per second, but you can switch to a different frame with the steps below:

1. In Settings app on your iPhone ◎, click **Camera.**

2. Click **Record Video** & choose the desired option.

Set Up ProRes Videos

This is for iPhone 15 Pro & Pro Max only. ProRes videos have less compression & higher color fidelity & can be used on all cameras. To set up,

1. In Settings app on your iPhone ◎, click **Camera.**

2. Click **Formats** & switch on **Apple ProRes.**

Record ProRes Video

1. Open the camera app then switch to Video mode, then press (ProRes) to switch ProRes on or press (ProRes) to switch it off.

2. Then press the Record button on your screen to start or stop recording.

Record QuickTake Video

Shoot videos and take photos at the same time.

1. Press & hold the camera ⭘ button in photo mode to start a QuickTake video recording.

2. Drag the ⃝ button to the right & release it over the lock to use the hands-free recording.

3. Press the ⃝ button for still photos while recording.

4. Press **Record** button to end the recording.

5. Click the thumbnail at the bottom of your screen to view the video.

Record in Cinematic Mode

This mode adds a special effect to your videos – it focuses on the subject & blurs the background. Although iPhone 15 detects the subject automatically, you can manually modify the camera focus.

1. Swipe to the **Cinematic** mode and press '1x' to zoom in before recording.

2. Press ⓕ to modify the special effect – use the slider to get the look you like.

3. Then press any of the volume buttons or Record button on your screen to start or stop recording.

4. While recording, a yellow frame will identify the subject while a gray frame shows the person isn't in focus. Press the gray box to switch the focus from one person to another, & tap it twice to lock the camera focus on the intended subject.

5. For videos without humans, press anywhere on your screen to set the focus.

6. Press & hold your screen to lock the lens focus at a single distance.

Record a Slow-Motion Video

This mode adds a slow-motion effect to your video.

1. Open the Camera app & swipe to **Slo-Mo** mode. Press ⟳ to use your front camera for the video.

2. Then press the Record button on your screen to start or stop recording.

You can choose to have a part of the video in slow motion & the remaining part at regular speed. To do this,

1. Click the thumbnail to open the video & press **Edit.**

2. Then use the bars under the frame viewer to set the parts that should remain in slow motion.

Record a Time-Lapse Video

Time-lapse video records an event over a period of time, like traffic flowing or someone running.

1. Open the Camera app & swipe to Time-lapse mode.

2. Position your iPhone 15 to capture the scene. Then press the Record button on your screen to start or stop recording.

Tip: positioning your iPhone 15 with a tripod will give the video more brightness & detail when recording in low-light conditions.

Quickly Change Video Frame Rate & Resolution

As against going into the iPhone 15 settings always, one quick way to change a video frame rate & resolution is through the quick toggles that will show at the top of your screen once enabled.

1. Press the quick toggles button in the upper right corner of your screen to switch between 4K or HD recording.

Adjust Auto FPS Settings

Your video quality is low when you record in a low-light environment. The iPhone 15 can improve the quality by automatically reducing the frame rate. To allow this,

1. In Settings app on your iPhone ⊚ , click **Camera.**

2. Click **Auto FPS** & choose to apply the setting to both 30- & 60-fps video or only 30-fps video.

Activate Prioritize Faster Shooting

This setting allows you to capture more photos on your iPhone 15 as you rapidly click the ◯ button. This setting is turned on by default.

To deactivate,

1. In Settings app on your iPhone ⊚ , click **Camera.**

2. Then switch off **Prioritize Faster Shooting.**

Save Camera Settings

Use any changes you made to the camera settings the next time you open the app.

1. In Settings app on your iPhone ⊚ , click **Camera.**

2. Click **Preserve Settings** & switch on the desired options.

Activate Camera Lock

This setting prevents the iPhone 15 from automatically switching between cameras when you are recording a video.

1. In Settings app on your iPhone ⊚ , click **Camera.**

2. Select **Record Video** & switch on **Lock Camera.**

Turn Stereo Recording On

iPhone 15 combines multiple microphones to give you the best stereo sound. To deactivate or activate stereo recording,

1. In Settings app on your iPhone ⦿ , click **Camera.**

2. Then switch off **Record Stereo Sound.**

Use Live Text with your Camera

Use your phone camera to read text in an image and open websites, make phone calls and other activities.

1. Position the text to show within your camera frame, & a yellow frame will show around the text.

2. Tap the ⊡ icon & select text by swiping or using the grab points.

3. Click on the appropriate option on your screen to perform an action: Copy, Look up, Select all, Translate, Share.

4. To make a call, visit a website, or start an email, press the phone number, website address, or email address on your screen.

5. Press the ⊜ button to go back to the camera app.

Switch off Lens Corrections

Lens corrections adds a more natural look to your photo. This setting is turned on by default. To deactivate,

1. In Settings app on your iPhone ⦿ , click **Camera.**

2. Then switch off **Lens Correction.**

PHOTO MANAGEMENT: ORGANIZING AND SHARING YOUR MEMORIES.

View Photos

Your photos are organized into different sections that you will find at the bottom of the Photo app screen.

1. Click on each tab to view its content.

2. Click on a photo to open it or a video to play it. Press & hold a Live Photo (has the ◎ icon) to play it.

3. Press ⓘ on the video or photo full screen view to view more details about the photo, like the date & time the photo was taken, the people in the photo, the location the photo was taken, & more.

4. Tap ‹ to return to the album.

Delete or Hide Video or Photos

1. Open the video or photo & press the 🗑 icon to delete the content from your phone.

2. Press the ⬆️icon to hide the content. The hidden content will only appear in the Hidden album.

You can also hide the hidden album with the steps below:

1. In Settings app on your iPhone ◎, click **Photo.**

2. Then switch off the **Hidden Album** button. Turn on the switch to see the album again.

Edit a Live Photo

You can mute sounds in a live photo, trim the length or change the main photo.

1. Press the ◎icon to make the following changes:

2. To choose one primary photo from the lots, move the white frame to the photo you want, & then press **Make Key Photo** & press **Done.**

3. To trim the photo length, drag one end of the frame viewer to select the frames for the Live Photo.

4. To turn the Live Photo into a still photo, press **Live** at the top of the screen. You would only see the key photo. Press Live again to undo.

5. Tap 🔊at the top of your screen to mute or unmute the photo.

6. Open the Live Photo in the Photos app & press **Edit.**

Play a Video

1. Click the video to play it. Then use the player controls at the bottom of the screen to delete, share, favorite, pause, mute, or see more details about the video.

2. Double press your screen to change from full screen to fit-to-screen.

3. Press & hold the frame viewer above the player controls to pause the video, then move the viewer slide right or left to fast-forward or rewind the video.

Permanently Delete or Recover Deleted Photos & Videos

You can recover your deleted photos or choose to permanently delete them off your device.

1. Open the Photos app & press **Albums,** then select **Recently Deleted** (you will find this under **Utilities).**

2. Press **Select,** click all the videos & photos you want, then click **Delete** or **Recover.**

Edit Photos & Videos

You can rotate, crop, add a filter, add color, & more to your photos & videos.

1. Open the photo or video you want to edit, & press **Edit.**

2. To adjust color & light, swipe under the photo to view the different effects, then click an effect to edit & use the slider to get the desired look.

3. To crop, flip or rotate, press ⊞ & then manually use the rectangle corners to choose the areas you want to retain or tap ⬛ to crop to a standard pre-set ratio on the iPhone 15

    Press ◼ to rotate a picture 90 degrees.
    Press ▲▲ to horizontally flip the picture.

DRAG IT TO TILT OR STRAIGHTEN

4. Press ⬥ to automatically add effects to your videos or photos.

5. To apply a filter, press ⊗, select the filter, & use the slider to modify the effect.

6. To write or draw on the photo, press Ⓐ & use the different colors & drawing tools to annotate your photo. Press ＋ to add text, captions, your signatures, or shapes.

7. Once you are satisfied with all the edits, press **Done.** Otherwise, press **Cancel** & select **Discard Changes.**

Revert an Edited Photo or Video

To return an edited photo or video to its original copy,

1. Open the photo or video & click **Edit.**

2. Select **Revert** & click **Revert to Original.**

Trim Video Length

Shorten the length of a video with the steps below:

1. Open the video & click **Edit.**

2. Drag one end of the frame viewer to change the stop or start times of the video.

3. Press **Done** & press **Save Video** to keep only the trimmed video, or press **Save Video as New Clip** to have both untrimmed & trimmed videos.

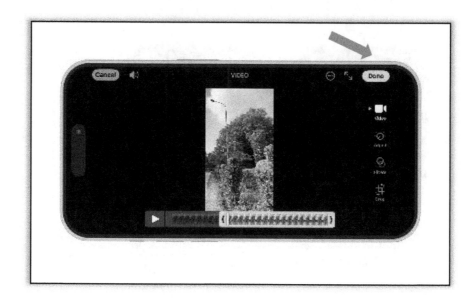

Turn Off the Cinematic effect in a Video

1. Open a video you shot in the Cinematic mode & press **Edit.**

2. Press **Cinematic** at the top of your screen & press **Done.** Do the same thing to return the cinematic effect.

Create a New Photo Album

Photo albums help you organize your photos. To create a new album,

1. Press **Albums** at the end of your screen.

2. Press ╋ & select **New Album.** Title your album & press **Save.**

3. Select all the photos & videos you want to move to the album & then press **Done.**

Rearrange, Rename & Delete Albums

1. Open **Photos** & click **Album** at the bottom of your screen.

2. Press **See All** & select **Edit.**

3. To rearrange, hold the album thumbnail & move it to a different location.

4. To rename, touch the album name & type in a new one.

5. To delete, press ⊖. Tap **Done** to finish.

Move Videos & Photos to an Existing Album

1. Open **Photos** & click **Library** at the bottom of your screen.

2. View **All Photos** or view by Days.

3. Press **Select** at the top & choose the content you want.

4. Tap the ⬆️ icon, select **Add to Album,** & click the desired album.

Remove Content from an Album

1. Open the album & click on a photo or video, press 🗑 & choose to delete only from the album or from the device.

2. To remove more than one item, press **Select,** choose the items, & tap 🗑.

Print Photos to an AirPrint-Enabled Printer

1. To print one video, open it, press ⬆️ & select **Print**.

2. To print more than one photo, click **Library,** press **All Photos,** press **Select,** & choose all the items you want to share. Press ⬆️& press **Print**.

Share Photos & Videos

1. To share one video or photo, open it, press ⬆️ & select a share option.

2. To share more than one content, click **Library,** press **All Photos,** press **Select,** & choose all the items you want to share. Press ⬆️& select a share option.

ICLOUD AND PHOTO STORAGE: KEEPING YOUR PHOTOS SAFE.

How iCloud Photos Operates

iCloud Photos effortlessly stores every photo and video you capture in iCloud, providing you with seamless access to your library across all devices at any time. Changes made to your collection on one device automatically synchronize with your other devices. Your media is systematically categorized into Years, Months, Days, and All Photos, ensuring easy retrieval. Memories, People & Pets, and other organizational elements are consistently updated across all platforms. This streamlined process facilitates quick searches for specific moments, family members, or friends.

All your photos and videos retain their original formats and full resolution in iCloud, encompassing formats such as HEIF, JPEG, RAW, PNG, GIF, TIFF, HEVC, MP4, and special formats unique to iPhone or iPad, like 4K videos, slo-mo, time-lapse, and Live Photos. The duration for your media to display on all devices and iCloud.com can vary based on your internet speed.

Enabling iCloud Photos

In order to enable iCloud Photos, you must first confirm that you have iCloud installed on all of your devices and then sign in using the same Apple ID. Using your iPhone, you can:

1. Navigate to Settings > [your name].

2. Tap iCloud.

3. Select Photos, then toggle the switch next to Sync this [device].

Editing or Deleting Photos

Edits and deletions made to photos or videos are instantly reflected across all connected devices.

> Edits are synchronized across all devices, allowing you to view changes made in the Photos app on your iPhone, iPad, or Mac, including Apple TV. Original photos and videos are securely stored in iCloud, allowing you to revert changes at any time. Deletions occur universally across all devices when performed on one. Accidentally deleted items can be recovered from the Recently Deleted folder within 30 days before being permanently removed.

Downloading Copies of Photos and Videos

When iCloud Photos is activated, media is automatically uploaded to iCloud without duplication in the backup. To download copies or import your library:

> On iCloud.com, select Photos, choose the desired media, and click the download button for the highest resolution or alternative formats.
> On your iPhone, use the Photos app to select content, tap the share button, and choose AirDrop for smaller quantities. For larger amounts, learn how to import photos.

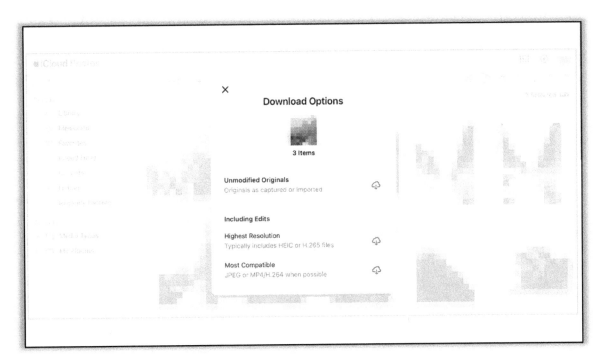

CREATIVE PHOTOGRAPHY: TIPS FOR CAPTURING LIFE'S MOMENTS.

Tips for taking the best photos with your iPhone 15 camera this Christmas season:

- Take advantage of the Portrait mode and the ability to edit depth and focus point to capture artistic photos.

- Consider using a light source in front of the subject to achieve better results. Smart HDR and metering exposure on iPhone 15 Pro can also help with overall exposure.

- Take advantage of the multiple lens options on the iPhone 15 Pro Max to capture different shots. Use wide camera for group portraits, and telephoto options for close-ups or shots of distant details.

- Use the macro mode to zoom in and capture a different and creative view. Pay attention to color and light to enhance the photo.

- Experiment with different color combinations to create striking photos. Mixing warm and cold tones or using complementary colors can add contrast to the scene.

- Use Live Photo to capture moments before and after taking a picture and create short videos that can be shared.

- Use aerial shots and the grid to compose still life photos with multiple elements or delicious plates of food. Keep in mind the camera level to ensure proper composition.

- Capture moments in slow motion with Slo-Mo video, such as people playing in the snow or pouring champagne.

- Don't forget to include yourself in portraits using the camera timer or Apple Watch Camera Control. Encourage interaction between people in the photos.

- Take multiple pictures to ensure the perfect shot and use iPhone Shortcuts to create a GIF easily.

Remember to have fun and be creative while capturing precious moments with your new iPhone 15 camera!

ORGANIZING YOUR DAILY LIFE

DIGITAL ASSISTANTS: USING ALARMS, TIMERS, AND REMINDERS.

Using alarms, timers, and reminders on your iPhone is easy and convenient, thanks to the built-in digital assistant, Siri, and the Clock and Reminders apps. Here's a guide on how to set up alarms, timers, and reminders:

Setting Alarms with Siri

1. **Activate Siri:** Press and hold the Side or Home button (depending on your iPhone model) until you hear the Siri activation sound or say "Hey Siri" if you have it enabled.

2. **Set an Alarm:** You can say commands like:

   - "Set an alarm for [time]."
   - "Wake me up at [time] tomorrow."
   - "Set an alarm for 7 AM."

3. **Check Alarms:** Ask Siri, "What alarms do I have set?"

Using the Clock App for Alarms

1. **Open the Clock App:** Locate the Clock app on your iPhone's home screen and open it.

2. **Set an Alarm:**

   - Tap on the "Alarm" tab at the bottom.
   - Tap on the "+" in the upper-right corner.
   - Set the time, choose repeat options, and tap "Save."

3. **Manage Alarms:** View, edit, or delete alarms from the "Alarm" tab.

3. Setting Timers with Siri:

1. **Activate Siri:** Press and hold the Side or Home button or say "Hey Siri."

2. **Set a Timer:** You can say commands like:

   - "Set a timer for [duration]."
   - "Set a timer for 10 minutes."
   - "Countdown 5 minutes."

3. **Check Timers:** Ask Siri, "How much time is left on my timer?"

4. Using the Clock App for Timers:

1. **Open the Clock App:** Open the Clock app from your home screen.

2. **Set a Timer:**
   - Tap on the "Timer" tab at the bottom.
   - Use the picker wheels to set the desired countdown time.
   - Tap "Start" to begin the timer.

3. **Manage Timers:** View, pause, resume, or reset timers from the "Timer" tab.

5. Setting Reminders with Siri:

1. **Activate Siri:** Press and hold the Side or Home button or say "Hey Siri."

2. **Set a Reminder:** You can say commands like:
   - "Remind me to [task] at [time]."
   - "Remind me to call [name] tomorrow."
   - "Add [task] to my reminders."

3. **Check Reminders:** Ask Siri, "What reminders do I have?"

6. Using the Reminders App:

1. **Open the Reminders App:** Find and open the "Reminders" app on your home screen.

2. **Set a Reminder:**
   - Tap the "+" in the upper-right corner.
   - Enter your reminder details, including title, date, and time.
   - Tap "Add."

3. **Manage Reminders:** View, edit, or mark reminders as completed within the "Reminders" app.

7. Location-Based Reminders:

1. **Use Siri or Reminders App:** You can set reminders based on your location. For example:
   - "Remind me to buy milk when I'm at the grocery store."
   - In the Reminders app, you can choose to add a location to a reminder.

Using these features, you can efficiently manage your time, stay on track with tasks, and make sure you never miss important events or appointments on your iPhone.

CALENDAR MANAGEMENT: KEEPING TRACK OF YOUR SCHEDULE.

Managing your schedule on the iPhone is easy and efficient with the built-in Calendar app. Here's a guide on how to keep track of your schedule, create events, and stay organized:

1. **Open the Calendar App:** Locate the Calendar app on your iPhone's home screen (it has an icon with a date and time).

2. **Viewing Your Calendar:** Every time you log in, the current month will be displayed. Swipe left or right to navigate between months. Tap "Today" in the bottom left to quickly return to the current date.

3. **Creating a New Event:**

   Tap the "+" sign at the top right to create a new event.
   Provide the following information regarding the event:
   - Title: Enter the name of the event.
   - Location: Add the event location.
   - Starts/Ends: Set the date and time for the event.
   - All-day: Toggle this switch if the event spans the entire day.
   Tap "Add" or "Done" to save the event.

4. **Editing an Event:** Tap on an existing event to open its details. Make changes as needed, then tap "Done" to save.

5. **Deleting an Event:** Open the event details. Scroll to the bottom then tap "Delete Event."

6. **Calendar Views:** At the bottom of the Calendar app, you can switch between various views: Day, Week, Month, and Year. Choose the one that suits your preference.

7. **Setting Reminders:** You can add reminders to your calendar events:

   Open the event details.
   Tap "Add Reminder."
   Set the reminder time.

8. **Sync with Other Calendars:** If you use other calendars (e.g., Google Calendar, Outlook), you can sync them with the iPhone Calendar app.

   - Go to Settings > Passwords & Accounts > Add Account.
   - Choose the account type and sign in to sync your calendar.

9. **Invitees and Shared Calendars:** When creating or editing an event, you can add invitees and share your calendar with others.

   - Tap "Add Invitees" or "Calendar" while editing an event.

10. **Time Zone Support:** If you frequently travel, you can enable Time Zone Support:

    o Go to Settings > Calendar > Turn on "Time Zone Override."

11. **Search for Events:** Tap the magnifying glass at the top left to search for specific events.

12. **Widget on Home Screen:** You can add the Calendar widget to your home screen for quick access to upcoming events.

    o Long-press on home screen, tap the "+" icon, find Calendar, and add the widget.

13. **Custom Calendar Colors:** You can assign different colors to different calendars:

    o Tap "Calendars" at the bottom of Calendar app.
    o Tap the color next to a calendar to choose a new one.

14. **Set Default Calendar:** You can choose a default calendar for new events:

    o Go to Settings > Calendar > Default Calendar.

15. **Notifications for Events:** Enable notifications to receive alerts before events:

    o Go to Settings > Calendar > Default Alert Times.

By utilizing these features in the Calendar app, you can efficiently manage your schedule, set reminders, and stay organized on your iPhone. Additionally, integrating other calendar accounts ensures that you have a comprehensive view of all your events and appointments.

NOTES AND RECORDS: STAYING ORGANIZED WITH YOUR IPHONE.

Staying organized on your iPhone is made easy with the Notes app and other built-in tools. Here's a guide on how to use Notes and other features to keep track of information and stay organized:

Using the Notes App

1. **Open the Notes App:** Locate the Notes app on your iPhone's home screen (it has an icon with a yellow notepad).

2. **Create a New Note:** Tap the "+" button in the bottom center to create a new note.

3. **Note Organization:** Create folders to organize your notes. Tap "Edit" in the top left corner and then "New Folder" to create one.

4. **Formatting Options:** Use formatting tools like bold, italics, and bullet points for better organization.

5. **Checklists:** Turn a note into a checklist by tapping the checklist button.

6. **Add Photos and Sketches:** Insert photos or create sketches within your notes for visual information.

7. **Share Notes:** Collaborate by sharing your notes with others. Tap the share icon and choose your sharing method.

8. **Search Notes:** Easily find specific notes by using the search bar at the top of the Notes app.

Scanning Documents with Notes

Open a note, tap the camera icon, then select "Scan Documents" to capture and organize paper documents.

Using the Files App

1. **Access Files:** Use the Files app to organize and access photos, documents, and other files on your iPhone.

2. **Create Folders:** Organize files into folders for better structure.

3. **iCloud Drive:** Store files in iCloud Drive for easy access across all your Apple devices.

HEALTH TRACKING: USING THE HEALTH APP FOR WELLNESS.

The Health app serves as a potent tool for tracking and overseeing your health and fitness. It accumulates data from diverse sources, encompassing your iPhone's sensors and compatible health and fitness devices. Here's how to make the most of the Health app:

Tracking Health Data

1. Open the Health app on your iPhone.

2. Tap "Browse" at the bottom to explore various health categories, including Activity, Nutrition, Sleep, and more.

Add Data

To manually add data, tap a category, then select **"Add Data"** or **"Add Data Point."** You can input information like your weight, blood pressure, or the number of steps you've taken.

Connect Devices

You can connect various health and fitness devices, like a smartwatch or fitness tracker, to the Health app. Data from these devices will be automatically collected and displayed.

Health Records

In some regions, you can access your health records, including lab results, medications, and immunizations, through the Health app. Check with your healthcare provider to enable this feature.

Set Health Goals:

To track and achieve health goals, tap "Summary" at the bottom, then "Get Started" under "Set Up Health Records" or select a specific health category.

Emergency Medical ID:

Set up your Emergency Medical ID by tapping "Summary," scrolling down, and selecting "Medical ID." This information can be accessed by emergency responders from your lock screen.

MONITORING MEDICATIONS

Health app is called "Medications," which can be accessed in two ways: by searching for "Medications" in the app's search box, or by browsing it in the Browse tab and scrolling down to it.

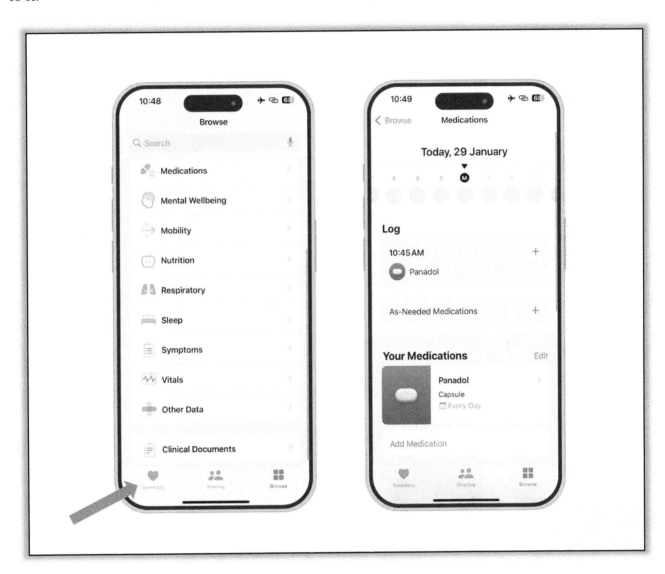

You can keep track of every drug, vitamin, and herb remedy you take with the help of the Medications app, which will then send you reminders when it's time to take your pills and analyze your data for any drug interactions.

In the Health app, selecting the Add Drug button is all that is required to add a new medication. There, you may search for a certain medication or vitamin by typing its name or scanning its label with your iPhone's camera. Scan-based addition is convenient, but it doesn't always capture all the data, so you may have to choose the dosage and form by hand (pill, spray, etc).

It's up to you from there how often you want to take medicine. You may schedule your prescription doses to be taken at any time of day, on any day of the week, or on an as-needed basis.

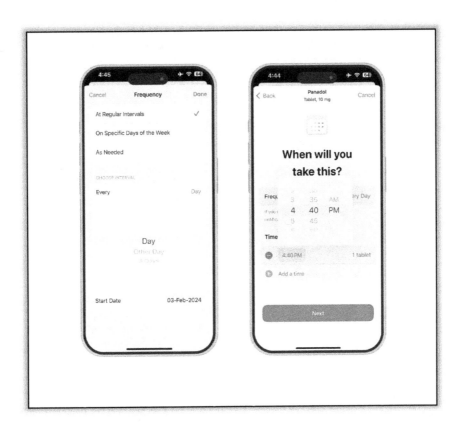

Medicines may be made to look like the actual pill you take, down to the color and form.

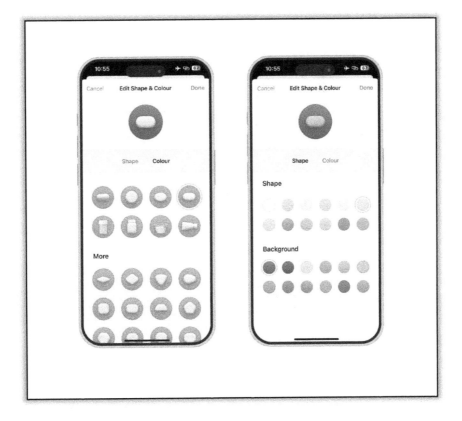

The Health app has a place for you to keep track of the vitamins and prescriptions you take.

Unless you change the option, medication reminders will be sent at the time you choose since they are considered time-sensitive alerts.

All drugs with a regular time and/or day have a reminder sent to you automatically.

Medication Logging

When a reminder alert appears, tapping it will open a window where you may choose "Taken" or "Skipped" for a drug. If many prescriptions are due at the same time, you may utilize the "Mark All as Taken" function. The Health app's medication list also allows you to record medications by checking the appropriate box.

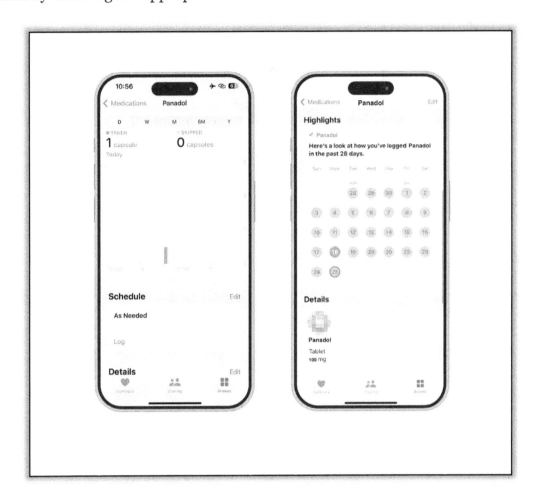

You may monitor your drug intake using the Health app over time to make sure you're taking your pills as prescribed. Information is presented daily, weekly, monthly, semiannual, and annual.

In addition to the Health summary, Apple will provide Medications "Highlight" that details how frequently a medicine has been taken over the last 28 days.

Apple Watch Medication App

WatchOS 9 has a Medications app specifically designed to make tracking your medications easier. The software allows you to record each dose taken separately or all at once by tapping "Log All as Taken." The "Skipped" option is used when a dosage has been missed.

All medication management should be done in the Health app; the Apple Watch app is just used to check off when pills have been taken.

Medication Interactions

The Health app performs frequent checks to ensure that the drugs you are taking do not interact with one another, preventing you from accidentally taking a harmful dose of more than one drug.

PERSONALIZING YOUR IPHONE EXPERIENCE

CUSTOMIZING YOUR HOME SCREEN: MAKING IT YOURS.

How to Add and Edit Widgets on Your Iphone's Home Screen

As you might be aware, if you have an iPhone, you can add widgets to Home Screen. If you touch and hold on any empty portion of the Home Screen, the apps will start jiggling. You'll find a plus (+) button at the top-right corner of the screen.

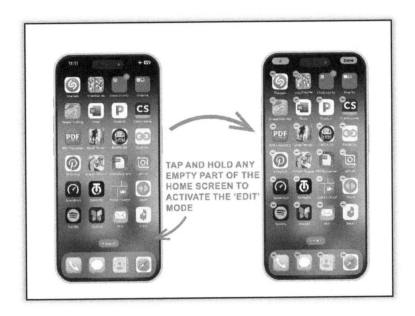

To add a widget, tap that plus (+) button. This will reveal the widget library, where you'll have access to several widgets you can choose from, ranging anywhere from Notes, Reminders, Fitness, News, Photos, and anything else you want.

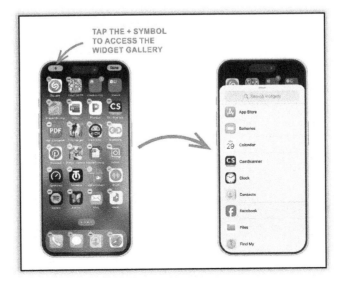

Essentially, you can choose and add any of the above-mentioned widgets (and more) to your Home Screen. So, for example, if you want to add a widget for your battery to your Home Screen, you can do it directly from the widget gallery. Tapping on any of the provided widget options will show the three standard sizes available to choose from. The small widget has a square icon. The medium-sized widget is rectangular in shape, and the final size is often the large one.

Immediately after you tap the "**Add Widget**" button below the size you want, your iPhone adds it to your Home Screen.

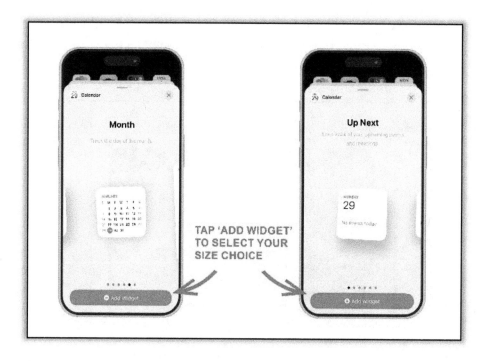

AFTER MAKING ALL
EDITS, TAP 'DONE'
TO SAVE THEM

Close an app on your iPhone

To clear apps that are open and running in the background on your iPhone, swipe up from the bottom of the screen to midway, and you'll see all the apps that are currently open on your iPhone at that time. To clear those running apps, swipe up on the respective app cards, and those apps will be closed.

SWIPE UP FEO THE
BOTTOM OF THE
HOME SCREEN TO
SEE OPENED APPS

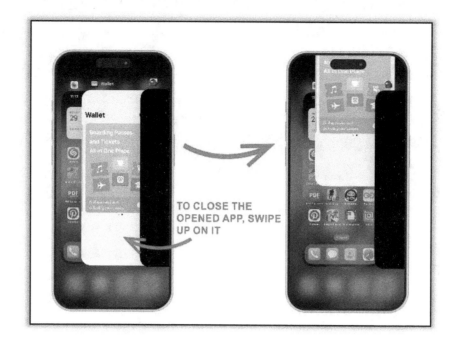

TO CLOSE THE OPENED APP, SWIPE UP ON IT

Make sure to do this frequently, as it is a way to save battery power and make your device run more smoothly, so you don't have all of these apps running at the same time, draining your battery.

Remove or Hide Apps from your iPhone's Home Screen

Also, if you hold down your Home Screen, you're going to see that the apps start to jiggle. They also have these minus buttons next to each app or widget on the Home Screen. If, for example, you're spending too much time on an app like Telegram, if you tap the minus (-) sign next to the Telegram app while your Home Screen is still in jiggle or "**Edit**" mode, you will have the option to delete the app or remove it from your iPhone's Home Screen.

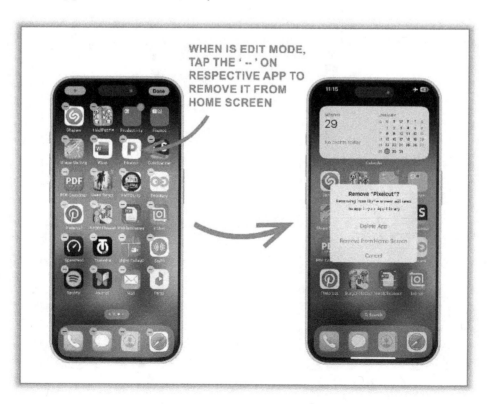

WHEN IS EDIT MODE, TAP THE ' -- ' ON RESPECTIVE APP TO REMOVE IT FROM HOME SCREEN

TAP 'DELETE APP' TO PERMANENTALY REMOVE THE APP FROM IPHONE

TAP 'REMOVE FROM HOME SCREEN' TO REMOVE IT DROM HOME SCREEN ONLY

Say you don't want to delete it because you like to spend some time on Telegram but it's affecting your productivity, you can remove the Instagram app from your Home Screen so that you don't see it, making you less inclined to use it often. If you select the "**Remove from Home Screen**" option, the app is not going to be on your Home Screen, but it will still be on your device.

To use the app again whenever you want, you can launch Spotlight, your iPhone's search tool, and then type in the app name. You can also find it in your iPhone's App Library. To open the App Library, swipe left through all your Home Screen pages to access the App Library.

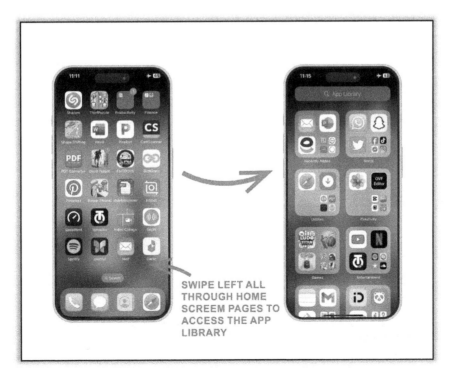

SWIPE LEFT ALL THROUGH HOME SCREEM PAGES TO ACCESS THE APP LIBRARY

Then type in the name of the application you seek in the search bar at the top of the screen.

You'll then be able to find any app that you've hidden from your Home Screen, provided it's still installed on your device.

How to Hide Home Screen App Pages on iPhone

If you have lots of Home Screen pages with several apps, you can actually hide certain pages of your Home Screen so that you don't have to keep scrolling to find the important and frequently-used apps. To do this,

1. Hold down the Home Screen to enable the "**Edit**" mode (or jiggle mode), and then tap the page indicator (small dots below the apps on the Home Screen). This will reveal all the Home Screen pages on your iPhone 15 in a minimized view.

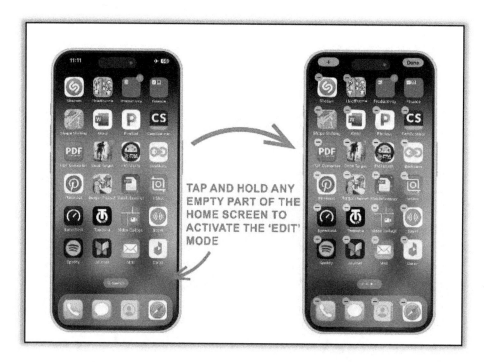

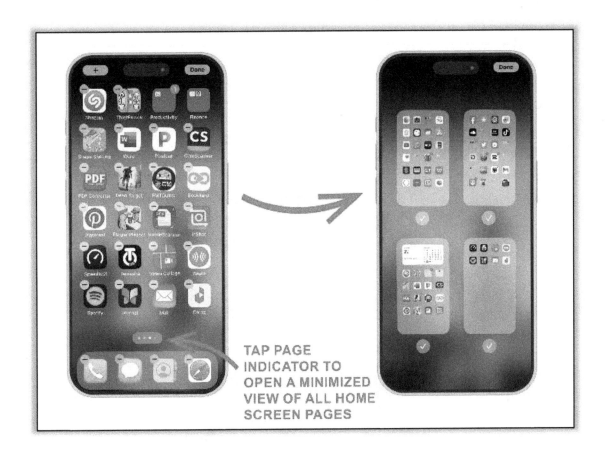

TAP PAGE INDICATOR TO OPEN A MINIMIZED VIEW OF ALL HOME SCREEN PAGES

2. Each Home Screen page has a check mark underneath. To hide any of these pages, uncheck the page.

UNCHECK ANY PAGE TO HIDE IT

3. Next, tap "**Done**" at the top-right corner of the screen to save your changes.

This will hide any unchecked pages. You can always bring back the page by repeating the process and then rechecking the page.

You can also delete the unchecked page. The apps on that Home Screen page will still be on your device, but they won't be available on the Home Screen.

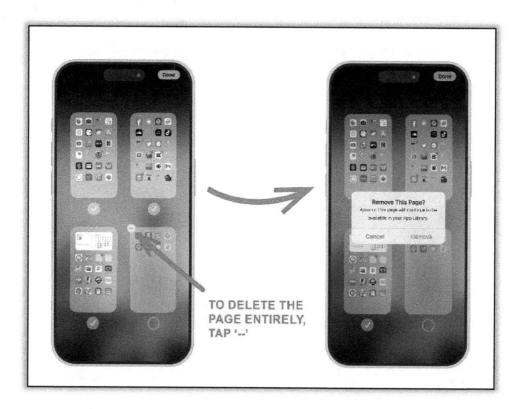

TO DELETE THE
PAGE ENTIRELY,
TAP '—'

You can use the Spotlight search feature or the App Library to access the apps on the deleted Home Screen page.

ADJUSTING DISPLAY AND SOUND: TAILORING YOUR SETTINGS.

Adjusting Display Brightness and Text Size

Your iPhone 15 offers a range of display settings that can be customized to suit your preferences & improve your overall user experience. Two of the most essential settings to personalize are display brightness and text size.

Adjusting Display Brightness:

The display brightness of your iPhone 15 can be adapted to various lighting conditions, ensuring that it's comfortable for your eyes and conserving battery life. Here's how to do it:

1. **Swipe Down from the Top Right Corner:** Begin by opening the Control Center by swiping down from the top right corner of your screen where you are now located.

2. **Adjust Brightness Slider:** In the Control Center, you'll find a brightness slider. Drag the slider left or right to decrease or increase the screen brightness. As you adjust the slider, the screen brightness will change accordingly.

3. **Auto-Brightness:** Your iPhone offers an "Auto-Brightness" feature that adapts the display brightness to ambient light conditions. To enable or disable it, go to "Settings" > "Display & Brightness" > "Auto-Brightness."

4. **Reduce White Point (Optional):** If you find the screen too bright even at the lowest brightness setting, you can further reduce brightness by enabling "Reduce White Point." This feature reduces intensity of bright colors on the screen. Go to "Settings" > "Accessibility" > "Display & Text Size" > "Reduce White Point."

5. **Night Shift and True Tone (Optional):** For enhanced display comfort, consider using features like "Night Shift" and "True Tone." "Night Shift" reduces blue light exposure at night, while "True Tone" adjusts the screen's white balance based on ambient lighting conditions. You can configure these options in "Settings" > "Display & Brightness."

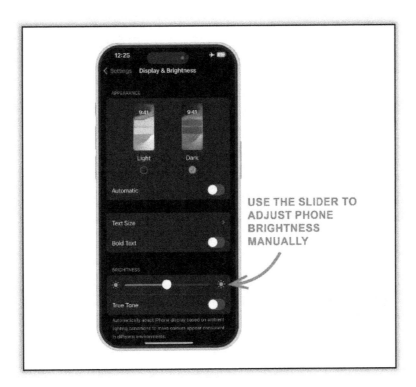

Adjusting Text Size:

Customizing text size on your iPhone 15 allows you to make text more readable and comfortable for your eyes. Follow these steps to modify text size:

1. **Go to Accessibility Settings:** Open the "Settings" app from your home screen.

2. **Access Display & Text Size:** Scroll down and tap "Accessibility." Then, tap "Display & Text Size."

3. **Adjust Text Size:** In the "Text Size" section, you'll see a slider that allows you to change the size of the text on your iPhone. Slide it to the left for smaller text or to the right for larger text. As you adjust the slider, you'll see a preview of the text size on the screen.

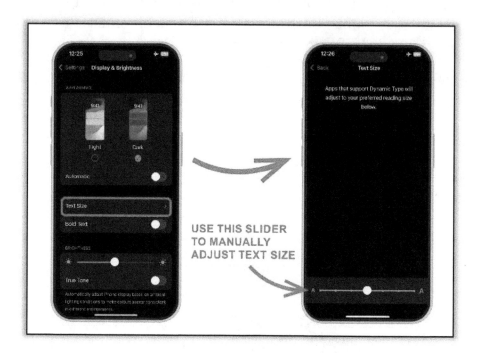

4. **Larger Accessibility Sizes:** If the text size slider doesn't provide a large enough text size for your needs, you can enable "Larger Accessibility Sizes" by tapping the toggle switch. This allows for even more significant adjustments.

5. **Bold Text (Optional):** To make text bolder and more distinct, you can enable the "Bold Text" option in the "Accessibility" settings. Keep in mind that enabling this feature will require your iPhone to restart.

6. **Dynamic Text (Optional):** Your iPhone also supports dynamic text that adjusts text size in supported apps, such as Messages and Mail. To enable this feature, go to "Settings" > "Accessibility" > "Display & Text Size" > "Larger Text." Here, you can configure the text size for supported apps.

7. **Switch to Bold Text (Optional):** If you have chosen to use a bolder text, you can do so by selecting "Settings" > "Display & Brightness" > "Text Size" and enabling the "Larger Accessibility Sizes." The iPhone will request a restart, and once it's back on, your text will be in bold.

Additional Tips for Display Customization:

To enhance your display experience further, consider the following tips:

1. **Dark Mode:** Use Dark Mode to switch to a darker color scheme, reducing eye strain and conserving battery life. You can enable Dark Mode in "Settings" > "Display & Brightness."

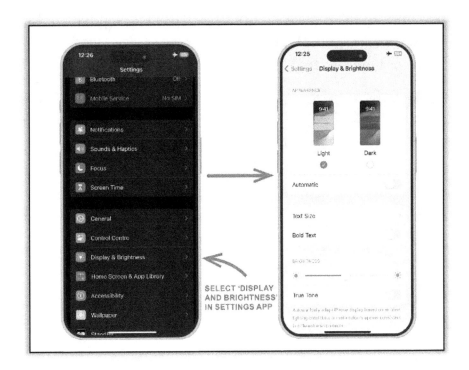

SELECT 'DISPLAY AND BRIGHTNESS' IN SETTINGS APP

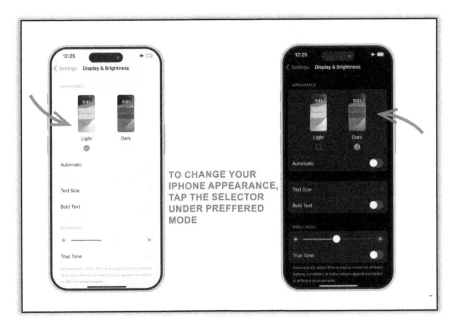

TO CHANGE YOUR IPHONE APPEARANCE, TAP THE SELECTOR UNDER PREFFERED MODE

2. **Reduce Motion:** To minimize screen animations and effects that may cause motion discomfort, navigate to "Settings" > "Accessibility" > "Motion" > "Reduce Motion."

3. **Color Filters (Optional):** For users with specific visual needs, the "Color Filters" feature in "Accessibility" settings allows you to modify the display's color palette. You can personalize it to align with your preferences.

4. **Increase Contrast (Optional):** If you require higher contrast for better visibility, "Increase Contrast" in "Accessibility" settings can help. It enhances the distinction between text and background.

5. **Accessibility Shortcut:** Consider configuring the "Accessibility Shortcut" to quickly toggle accessibility features, such as invert colors, grayscale, or color filters, by triple-clicking the side or home button.

6. **Custom Display Presets:** Some iPhones offer display presets like "Standard" and "Vivid" in "Settings" > "Display & Brightness" > "Display Presets." Experiment with these presets to see which one suits your visual preferences.

Changing Ringtone and Notification Sounds

CHANGING THE RINGTONE

1. **Open the Settings App:** Start by opening the "Settings" app from your home screen. It's represented by a gear or cogwheel icon.

2. **Scroll and Select "Sounds & Haptics":** In Settings menu, scroll down and tap "Sounds & Haptics." This option allows you to configure sound settings for your device.

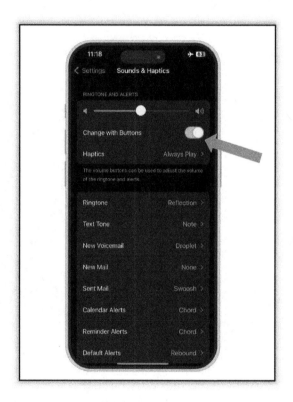

3. **Change the Ringtone:** Under the "Sounds and Vibration Patterns" section, you'll see various sound settings. To change your ringtone, tap "Ringtone." This will open a list of available ringtones.

4. **Select a New Ringtone:** Browse through the list of ringtones and tap on the one you'd like to set as your new ringtone. You can tap on a ringtone to preview it before making your selection.

5. **Confirmation:** After selecting a new ringtone, your choice will be highlighted, and you'll hear a preview of the selected ringtone.

1. **Open the Settings App:** Launch the "Settings" app on your iPhone 15.

2. **Scroll and Select "Sounds & Haptics":** In Settings menu, scroll down to "Sounds & Haptics."

3. **Change Notification Sounds:** Under the "Sounds and Vibration Patterns" section, you'll find various settings for different types of notifications. To customize a specific notification sound, tap on the respective option, such as "Text Tone" for messages or "New Mail" for email notifications.

4. **Select a New Sound:** Within the notification settings, tap on the specific notification sound (e.g., "Text Tone"). You'll see a list of available notification sounds.

5. **Choose Your Sound:** Browse through the list and tap on the sound you want to use for that notification. Like with ringtones, you can tap on a sound to preview it.

6. **Confirmation:** After selecting a new notification sound, your choice will be highlighted, and you'll hear a preview of the selected sound.

Adding Custom Ringtones and Sounds

If the built-in ringtones and notification sounds don't suit your preferences, you can add custom sounds to your iPhone:

1. **Prepare Your Custom Sound:** You'll need the custom sound in a compatible format (usually M4R for ringtones, and M4A or MP3 for notification sounds). Make sure it's saved to your iPhone or iCloud Drive.

2. **Add a Custom Ringtone:**

   a. Open the "Settings" app.

   b. Scroll down and select "Sounds & Haptics."

   c. Tap "Ringtone."

   d. Scroll down to the "Ringtones" section and you'll see a "Tone Store" option. Tap on it to browse and purchase ringtones from the iTunes Store.

   e. To add custom ringtones, open the "Files" app, navigate to the folder where your custom ringtone is saved, and tap on it. It will be added to your iPhone's ringtone list.

3. **Add Custom Notification Sounds:**

   a. Open the "Settings" app.

   b. Scroll down and select "Sounds & Haptics."

c. To add custom notification sounds, open the "Files" app, navigate to the folder where your custom notification sound is saved, and tap on it. It will be added to your iPhone's list of available notification sounds.

FACE ID SETUP

On the Face ID setup page, tap "**Continue**" and then follow the on-screen directions to activate it. You can tap "**Set Up Later in Settings**" if you wish to skip the setup for now.

SET A PASSCODE

Input any six-figure passcode of your choosing in the "**Passcode**" setup screen. However, make sure it is one you can easily remember. Next, enter the passcode again.

LOG IN YOUR APPLE ID

Input your existing Apple ID (if you have one), then tap the "**Next**" button. Utilize the **"Forgot password"** tab that is located within the Apple ID setup screen in the event that you have forgotten either the Apple ID or the password. To establish a new Apple ID, you can also create one by tapping the button that says **"don't have an Apple ID."** Next, enter the password for your Apple ID, and then select the **"Next"** button to continue.

NOTIFICATIONS: MANAGING ALERTS AND DISTRACTIONS.

Find Your Notifications

All notifications are in the notification center. Go to the notification center with the steps below

1. Swipe upward from the middle of the lock screen or from the top center of other screens. Then scroll to see any notification.

2. Swipe upward from the bottom of your iPhone 15 screen with one finger to close the page.

Receive Government Alerts

Note that this service is not available in all regions and countries.

1. In Settings app on your iPhone 〇 , click **Notifications.**

2. Scroll down to the list in the Government Alerts space & switch on the desired services.

Respond to Notifications

Notifications are grouped according to the sending apps for easy management. You will find the most recent notifications at the top of the notification center.

1. Tap a staked notification to exp& the list & view each notification individually. Click **Show Less** to close the group.

2. Press & hold a notification to view it & perform quick actions if available.

3. Click the notification to open the app that has the notification.

Manage Notifications

View your notifications, open the sending apps, clear them or mute them. See the steps below:

1. If you receive a notification while using another app, pull down the notification to view it & then swipe upward to dismiss it.

2. To clear notifications in the notification center, swipe left on a single or group notifications, then press **Clear** or **Clear All.**

3. To mute all notifications from a specific app, find a notification from that app, swipe left, select **Options,** & then use the appropriate mute option to mute notifications from that app for a specified hour or day. New notifications from the app will go straight to the Notification center without making any sounds or lighting up your screen.

To unmute, swipe left on a notification from that app in the Notification Center, select **Options,** & press **Unmute.**

1. To stop receiving notifications for an app, find a notification from that app, swipe left, select **Options,** & tap **Turn Off.**

2. To change how notifications from an app are displayed, find a notification from that app, swipe left, select **Options,** & then press **View Setting.**

3. To clear every notification in the notification center, press ⊗ & select **Clear.**

4. Switch on **Do Not Disturb** to mute all notifications.

Schedule Notification Summary

Rather than getting individual notifications, you can customize the iPhone to group the notifications and send them as a summary. This will help reduce distractions coming from notifications. In the setting, you will choose the notifications that should be in the summary and when you want to receive the summary.

1. In Settings app on your iPhone ◉ , click **Notification.**

2. Select **Scheduled Summary** & then switch on the **Scheduled Summary** switch.

3. Now choose all the apps to be included in the summary & set a time to receive the summary.

4. Click **Add Summary** to create another schedule.

5. Press **A to Z** to check that all the apps you want for the summary are switched on.

Show New Notifications on the Lock Screen

See recent notifications on your lock screen.

1. In Settings app on your iPhone ⊚ , click **Face ID & Passcode.**

2. Type in your passcode when prompted, then switch on **Notification Center** under **Allow Access When Locked.**

Change Notification Settings

The notification setting allows you to select the apps that can send notifications and customize sounds for incoming notifications.

1. In Settings app on your iPhone ⊚ , click **Notifications.**

2. To customize when you want to receive the most notification preview, click **Show Previews** & select an option: **When Locked, Always,** or **Never.** Tap ❮ to return to the previous screen.

3. To enable or disable notification for an app, click the app under **Notification Style,** & turn on or off the **Allow Notifications** switch. If you turned on the switch, you would need to choose the delivery time for notifications – immediately or following the set schedule.

4. To choose how notifications should be grouped, click **Notification Grouping** & select an option:

   o **By App** – groups all notifications from the same app.
   o **Automatic** – group notifications from an app according to the organizing criteria within that app.
   o **Off** – disable notification grouping.

You can also turn off notifications for select apps. To do this,

1. In Settings app on your iPhone ⊚ , click **Notifications.**

2. Click **Siri Suggestions** & then disable the desired apps.

Set up Location-based Alerts

This setting ties notifications from some apps to a specific location. For example, you can get a reminder to call a contact when you arrive at a specified location. To disable or enable this option,

3. In Settings app on your iPhone ⊚ , click **Privacy.**

4. Select **Location Services** & switch on **Location Services.**

Select an app in the list & then choose to share your location with that app while using the app.

OVERCOMING COMMON CHALLENGES

TROUBLESHOOTING TIPS: SOLVING COMMON IPHONE ISSUES.

Encountering issues with your iPhone can be frustrating, but many common problems have simple solutions. Here are some troubleshooting tips for addressing common iPhone issues:

Device Won't Turn On:

1. Charge your iPhone using the original charging cable and adapter.

2. Perform a force restart on your iPhone by swiftly pressing then releasing the volume up button, followed by the volume down button. Subsequently, press and hold the side (or home) button until the Apple logo is displayed.

Apps Crashing or Freezing:

1. Update app to the latest version from the App Store.

2. Restart your iPhone.

3. Delete and reinstall the problematic app.

Slow Performance:

1. Close background apps by swiping up from the bottom and swiping away the apps.

2. Clear storage space by removing unnecessary apps, photos, or videos.

3. Restart your iPhone.

Wi-Fi Connection Issues:

1. Toggle Wi-Fi off and on.

2. Forget the Wi-Fi network in Settings > Wi-Fi and reconnect.

3. Restart your router.

4. Reset network settings on your iPhone in Settings > General > Reset > Reset Network Settings.

Bluetooth Connection Problems:

1. Toggle Bluetooth off and on.

2. Forget the Bluetooth device in Settings > Bluetooth and reconnect.

3. Restart your iPhone.

No Sound or Low Volume:

1. Check if your iPhone is in silent mode by toggling the switch on the side.

2. Increase the volume using the volume buttons.

3. Ensure the speaker or headphone jack is not blocked.

Touchscreen Not Responding:

1. Clean screen with a soft, lint-free cloth.

2. Restart your iPhone.

3. If the issue persists, update your iPhone to the latest iOS version.

Battery Draining Quickly:

1. Check battery usage in Settings > Battery to identify power-hungry apps.

2. Disable background app refresh for unnecessary apps.

3. Adjust screen brightness and enable Low Power Mode.

Unable to Update iOS:

1. Connect to a Wi-Fi network.

2. Ensure your iPhone has sufficient storage space.

3. Restart your iPhone.

4. Try updating through iTunes on a computer.

iCloud Sync Issues:

1. Check your iCloud storage status.

2. Sign out of iCloud and sign back in.

3. Ensure iCloud services are not experiencing outages.

Camera Not Working:

1. Restart your iPhone.

2. Clear the camera lens of any obstructions.

3. Update your iPhone to latest iOS version.

Unable to Receive Calls or Texts:

1. Ensure that Do Not Disturb (DND) mode is not activated.

2. Check for network signal and confirm that your phone number is active with your carrier.

3. Restart your iPhone.

Face ID or Touch ID Issues:

1. Ensure your face or fingerprint is correctly registered in Settings > Face ID & Passcode or Touch ID & Passcode.

2. Clean the Face ID or Touch ID sensor.

3. Restart your iPhone.

iPhone Overheating:

1. Remove the case, if applicable, as it may contribute to overheating.

2. Close background apps.

3. Avoid using your iPhone in direct sunlight or extreme temperatures.

General Software Glitches:

1. Restart your iPhone.

2. Update to the latest iOS version.

3. If the issue persists, consider a factory reset after backing up your data.

If you've tried the solutions above and your iPhone issue persists, it may be worthwhile to contact Apple Support or visit an Apple Store for further assistance. Always ensure your data is backed up before attempting any troubleshooting steps that involve resetting or restoring your device.

KEEPING YOUR IPHONE UP-TO-DATE: UPDATES AND BACKUPS.

Automatically Update iPhone's iOS

Turn on automatic updates with the steps below:

1. In Settings app on your iPhone ⚙ , click **General.**

2. Select **Software Update** & click **Automatic Updates.**

3. Then switch on '**Download iOS Updates**' & '**Install iOS Updates.**'

When you switch on this option, the iPhone will search for and install new updates at night when your device is charging & connected to Wi-Fi.

Manually Update iPhone's iOS

1. In Settings app on your iPhone 🌐 , click **General.**

2. Select **Software Update** to check for any new updates.

3. Click any available update to download & install it.

Back up iPhone 15 using iCloud

This is one of the ways to back up your iPhone

1. In Settings app on your iPhone 🌐 , click your name.

2. Select **iCloud** & click **iCloud Backup.**

3. Switch on **iCloud Backup** & tap **Back Up Now** to manually back up your iPhone 15. Otherwise, iCloud will automatically back up your device daily when the device is locked, connected to Wi-Fi, & powered.

Back Up your iPhone 15 Using Windows PC

1. Connect your computer & your iPhone 15 with a cable.

2. Install & open the iTunes app, then tap the iPhone 15 tab close to the upper left side of the iTunes window.

3. Click **Summary** & select **Back Up Now.**

Back up your iPhone 15 Using Mac

1. Connect your Mac & your iPhone 15 with a cable.

2. Open the Finder sidebar on your Mac & click your iPhone 15

3. Click **General** at the top of that screen, then choose **"Back up all of the data on your iPhone 15 to this Mac."**

4. Then select **'Back Up Now.'**

GETTING HELP: USING APPLE SUPPORT AND RESOURCES.

If you need help with your iPhone or have questions about Apple products and services, there are several resources available to you. Here's a guide on how to use Apple support and resources using your iPhone:

Apple Support App:

Download the App:

1. Open the App Store on your iPhone.

2. Search for "Apple Support" and download the official Apple Support app.

Use the App:

1. Open the Apple Support app.

2. Sign in with your Apple ID.

3. Tap on the relevant product or issue.

4. Follow the on-screen prompts to get assistance.

Apple Support Website:

Visit the Website:

1. Open Safari or any other web browser on your iPhone.

2. Go to the official Apple Support website.

Navigate and Search: Use the search bar to find solutions to common problems or browse through topics related to your issue.
Contact Support: If you can't find the answer, there are options to contact Apple Support through chat or phone.

Contact Apple Support via Phone:

Call Apple Support: Dial 1-800-APL-CARE (1-800-275-2273) in the US. If you're in another country, check the official Apple Support page for the local support number.
Express Lane: Visit the Apple Support website, click on "Contact Support," and go through the Express Lane for faster service.

Apple Communities:

Visit Apple Communities:

1. Open Safari or any other web browser.

2. Go to the Apple Communities.

Search and Ask Questions: Use the search bar to find discussions related to your issue or join the community to ask questions.

Apple Store:

Visit an Apple Store:

1. Find the nearest Apple Store using the Apple Store app or Maps.

2. Schedule an appointment or visit the Genius Bar for in-person assistance.

Social Media:

Twitter and Facebook: Apple Support is active on Twitter (@AppleSupport) and Facebook. You can reach out to them through these platforms.

Feedback and Bug Reporting:

Provide Feedback: If you encounter issues or have suggestions, you can use the "Feedback" option in the settings or the Feedback Assistant app to report problems directly to Apple.

Remember to have your device information and Apple ID details ready when seeking support. Apple's support options may evolve, so it's a good idea to check the official Apple Support page for the latest information and resources.

ADVANCED SETTINGS: EXPLORING FURTHER CUSTOMIZATIONS.

Exploring advanced settings on your iPhone allows you to customize your device to better suit your preferences and needs. While iOS is designed to be user-friendly, there are several hidden or less obvious settings that you can adjust for a more personalized experience. Here are some advanced settings and customizations you can explore on your iPhone:

Accessibility Settings:

Settings > Accessibility:

1. Explore various accessibility features like VoiceOver, Magnifier, Display & Text Size, and more.

2. Enable features like AssistiveTouch for additional control options.

Privacy Settings:

Settings > Privacy:

1. Review and manage app permissions for Location Services, Camera, Microphone, Contacts, and more.

2. Check the "Tracking" section to control app tracking.

Keyboard Settings:

Settings > General > Keyboard:

1. Customize keyboard settings, such as Keyboards (add or remove), Key Flicks, and Shortcuts.

2. Explore the Text Replacement feature for creating custom shortcuts.

Notifications:

Settings > Notifications:

1. Adjust notification settings for each app individually.

2. Explore "Focus" settings for customizing notifications based on your activity.

Mail Settings:

Settings > Mail:

1. Configure advanced email settings, including Signature, Swipe Options, and more.

2. Adjust settings for individual email accounts.

Safari Settings:

Settings > Safari:

1. Customize Safari behavior, including search engine, privacy settings, and content blockers.

2. Manage website settings for specific preferences.

Background App Refresh:

Settings > General > Background App Refresh:

1. Control which apps can refresh content in the background.

2. Optimize battery usage by adjusting app refresh settings.

Cellular Data Settings:

Settings > Cellular:

1. Monitor data usage for each app.

2. Enable or disable cellular data for specific apps.

Storage & iCloud Usage:

Settings > General > [Device] Storage: Manage storage, view app-specific usage, and optimize storage by enabling features like Offload Unused Apps.

Face ID/Touch ID & Passcode:

Settings > Face ID & Passcode or Touch ID & Passcode:

1. Adjust Face ID/Touch ID settings.

2. Customize passcode options and app access.

App-Specific Settings:

Settings > [App Name]: Explore settings within individual apps for additional customization options.

Developer Settings:

Settings > Developer: If you have a developer account, you can access additional settings for debugging and testing.

Shortcuts App:

Shortcuts App (if installed): Create and customize automation shortcuts for various tasks.

Reset and System Options:

Settings > General > Reset: Explore options for resetting different aspects of your device if needed (e.g., Reset All Settings, Erase All Content and Settings).

ADVANCED TIPS AND TRICKS

SIRI: YOUR PERSONAL ASSISTANT.

Siri is your personal voice assistant, always ready to help you perform tasks and answer questions. Here's how to make the most of Siri:

1. **Activating Siri:** To activate Siri, simply say, "Hey Siri," or press then hold the Side button on your iPhone. You can also enable voice activation by going to "Settings" > "Siri & Search" and turning on "Listen for 'Hey Siri.'"

2. **Sending Messages:** Use Siri to send text messages or iMessages by saying, "Hey Siri, send a message to [contact's name]." Siri will prompt you to dictate your message.

3. **Setting Reminders and Alarms:** You can ask Siri to set reminders or alarms for specific tasks or events. For instance, "Hey Siri, set a reminder for 3 p.m. to call the doctor."

4. **Making Calls:** Dial contacts or phone numbers hands-free with Siri. Say, "Hey Siri, call [contact's name]" or "Hey Siri, call [phone number]."

5. **Checking the Weather:** Find out the weather forecast for your location or any other city by asking Siri, "What's the weather like today in [city]?"

6. **Setting Appointments:** Siri can schedule appointments and events for you. Try, "Hey Siri, schedule a meeting at 2 p.m. tomorrow."

7. **Opening Apps:** Open apps using voice commands. For instance, "Hey Siri, open Safari."

8. **Math and Conversions:** Ask Siri to perform calculations or unit conversions. "Hey Siri, what's 15% of 350?" or "Hey Siri, convert 30 miles to kilometers."

9. **General Knowledge:** Siri is a wealth of general knowledge. Inquire about historical events, ask for fun facts, or have Siri define words.

ADVANCED ACCESSIBILITY: ENHANCING USABILITY.

Enhancing usability on the iPhone 15 for individuals with accessibility needs involves leveraging the advanced accessibility features provided by Apple. Here are some tips & features that can enhance the usability of the iPhone 15 for users with diverse accessibility requirements:

VoiceOver:

Customization: Customize VoiceOver settings under Settings > Accessibility > VoiceOver. Adjust speaking rate, pitch, and other options to suit individual preferences.
Braille Support: Enable Braille support for users who are blind or have low vision under Settings > Accessibility > VoiceOver > Braille.

Magnifier:

Triple-Click Accessibility Shortcut: Set up a triple-click shortcut for the Magnifier. Go to Settings > Accessibility > Accessibility Shortcut and choose Magnifier. This allows quick access to the Magnifier feature by triple-clicking the side or home button.

Display & Text Size:

Text Size and Bold Text: Adjust text size and enable Bold Text for better readability under Settings > Display & Brightness > Text Size.
Larger Text: Enable Larger Accessibility Sizes for further customization.

Color Filters:

Customize Display: Adjust color filters to enhance visibility for users with color vision deficiencies. Find this feature under Settings > Accessibility > Display & Text Size > Color Filters.

Siri Shortcuts:

Custom Voice Commands: Create custom Siri Shortcuts to perform specific actions using voice commands. This can be especially useful for users with motor disabilities. Access this feature in Settings > Siri & Search > Siri Shortcuts.

AssistiveTouch:

Custom Gestures: Configure custom gestures and use the on-screen touch interface with AssistiveTouch. Find this feature under Settings > Accessibility > Touch > AssistiveTouch.

Subtitles & Captioning:

Customize Captions: Adjust subtitle and caption settings under Settings > Accessibility > Subtitles & Captioning. Enable closed captions and customize the appearance to enhance usability for users with hearing impairments.

Sound Recognition:

> **Alerts for Specific Sounds:** Enable Sound Recognition under Settings > Accessibility > Sound Recognition. This feature can notify users about specific sounds like doorbells, sirens, or alarms, benefiting those with hearing impairments.

Face ID and Attention Awareness:

> **Adjust Face ID:** Users can adjust Face ID settings to make facial recognition more accommodating. Go to Settings > Face ID & Passcode to find these options.

Switch Control:

> **Customize Switches:** For users with limited mobility, Switch Control allows the use of external adaptive devices. Customize switch input settings under Settings > Accessibility > Switch Control.

Remember that accessibility needs can vary widely, so it's essential to explore the various settings and features on the iPhone 15 to find the combination that works best for individual users. Additionally, staying informed about updates and new accessibility features from Apple is crucial for ensuring ongoing support.

OPTIMIZING BATTERY LIFE: PROLONGING PERFORMANCE.

This setting stops the iPhone from charging beyond 80% to preserve the battery life. It studies your use and only charges the iPhone to 100% on days it calculates that you need the full battery based on your previous usage data.

1. In Settings app on your iPhone ⚙, click **Battery** & select **Battery Health.**

2. Then switch on **Optimized Battery Charging.**

Charge the Battery

Using a USB-C cable and a power adapter that is compatible with the USB-C standard, including USB Power Delivery, you will have no trouble charging your iPhone 15. Most notably, this cable is typically included with your iPhone, making it readily accessible for charging. These cables and compatible power adapters are broadly available from Apple and various other manufacturers.

Here's how to charge your iPhone 15:

1. Connect the USB-C cable to the USB-C port on your iPhone.

2. Attach the other end of the cable to a USB-C power adapter that is compatible with your device.

3. Plug power adapter into a wall outlet.

If you happen to possess a 20W USB-C power adapter or one with a higher wattage rating, such as the adapter that came with your Mac laptop, you can use it to charge your iPhone. This will result in faster charging. You also have the option of charging your iPhone by connecting it to the USB-C connector that is contained within your computer.

By following these simple steps, you'll keep your iPhone 15 powered up and ready for action.

Review the Battery Health

Follow the steps below to see data about your battery peak performance, capacity, & when the battery needs servicing:

1. In Settings app on your iPhone ⊚ , click **Battery,** & select **Battery Health.**

Turn on Low Power Mode

I would recommend you use this feature when you have low battery and are not close to electrical power. It helps to preserve your battery life for as long as possible by reducing background activities and allowing you access to just basic features on your phone. To turn on.

1. In Settings app on your iPhone ⊚ , click **Battery,** & switch on **Low Power Mode.**

The iPhone 15 will automatically return to normal power mode when your battery level gets to 80%

Show Battery Percentage

To see your battery percentage,

1. Swipe from top-right corner of your screen down to see the percentage in the status bar.

See Battery Usage Data

This report will help you see apps that drain your battery and help you know the apps to reduce their usage and the ones to delete if possible.

1. In Settings app on your iPhone ⊚ , click **Battery.**

2. Go through each section to view different information regarding the battery.

Add Battery Widgets to Home Screen

Add this widget to your home screen so that you can view your battery percentage and usage right on the home screen page.

1. Press & hold the home screen background till the apps start to jiggle.

2. Press ➕ near the top of the screen, move down, & press **Batteries,**

3. Swipe to your left & right to see the different sizes – each size shows different information.

4. When you see the one you like, click **Add Widget** & press **Done.**

EXPLORING ADVANCED IPHONE FEATURES: BEYOND THE BASICS.

Make Notifications into A List Again

For the home screen, one more modification! You may use a list instead of the stacked notifications if you like them. Select List by going to Settings, Notifications, and Display As.

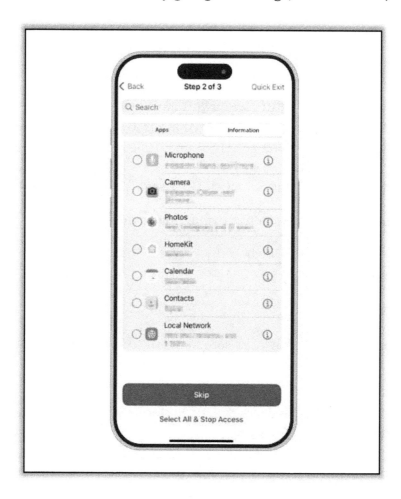

Audit what apps are accessing your data.

In order to enable individuals in perilous or abusive circumstances to know who may access their data and take appropriate action, Apple implemented a much-needed safety feature. Everyone should check out this option called Safety Check, which serves as quick security and privacy assessment. It will display the individuals and applications that have access to your microphone, camera, and location.

Access Safety Check by going to Settings Privacy & Security (near the bottom of the page). Go through the recommended check by tapping Manage Sharing & Access, then tapping Continue. The app list is organized to make it simpler to view and restrict access to applications. It is comparable to current Privacy & Security options.

Make Your Keyboard Vibrate, Quietly

When using the on-screen keyboard, get a delightful clicking sensation. By switching the on Haptic option to green, go to Settings Sounds & Haptics Keyboard Feedback.

(If your keyboard produces audible clicking noises as you type, this is not how you must live. Toggle the Sound option off there so that it is gray.)

Make Voice Calls to End Them.

You may now end a phone conversation without pressing a button if you want to converse while knitting or walking. Access Settings, Siri & Search, and Call. Hang up and turn on the switch. The next time you're on a phone or FaceTime call, sternly command Siri to end the conversation. Excellent for claiming the last word.

Dictate Emoji

Emojis may now be included in essential emails and texts that you dictate to your employer without having to edit them, afterwards. Say the desired emoji out loud, then the phrase "emoji." For instance: "Sad face emoji since the presentation won't be done on time." (This is compatible with iPhone XS and later.)

Get Rid of The Search Button

You no longer need to drag your finger down from the top of the screen to search for an app or contact since there is a little Search button at the bottom of your home screen. Toggle off the Show on Home Screen option under Search in Settings Home Screen if you don't like it.

Create Real-Time Captions

Even if the new function isn't as effective as genuine captions, it may still be helpful. Live captions will display a black box at the bottom of the screen that makes an effort to create captions for any open apps, including TikTok, podcasts, and your own videos.

View and Exchange Stored Wi-fi Passwords.

For some time now, Apple has enabled iOS users to share Wi-Fi passwords, but only when 2 Apple devices are in close proximity.

Moreover, accessing the password directly from your settings was not possible if the automatic function did not operate.

Additionally, you were required to recall the password if you wanted to share a stored Wi-Fi password with someone using a different platform, like an Android user or someone on a PC. That changes now.

Press the small information icon located on the right side of the network you desire in the Wi-Fi section of Settings. Access the Password field and utilize Face ID or enter your passcode to reveal the network password. The password may then be shared by tapping Copy once it has been copied to your clipboard.

Locate and Eliminate Duplicate Images and Videos.

Perhaps you downloaded a film more than once or saved the same picture more than once, leaving copies all throughout your photo album. If you have enough capacity, it may not be an issue, but if you're out of room, iOS 17 makes it simple to eliminate every identical file.

You ought to notice a new Duplicates album under Utilities under Photos > Albums. Apple scans your entire photo library, presenting every image or video that exists in duplicate within a specific album. You can then opt to eliminate duplicate items individually or simply press Merge to retain the superior image along with its associated data, discarding the duplicates.

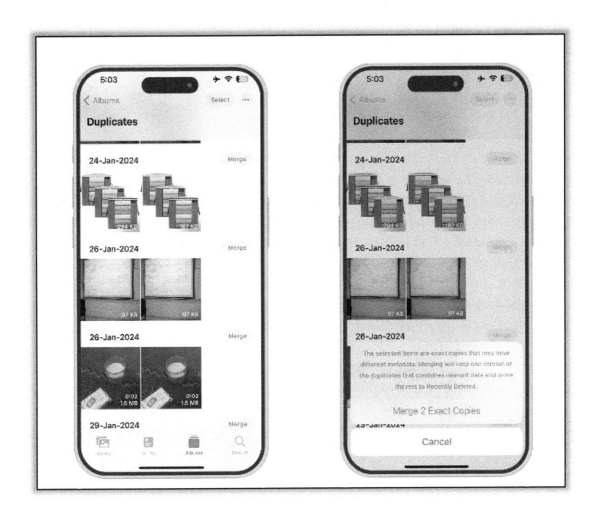

Utilize the Select > Select All > Merge option to efficiently remove all images and videos identified as duplicates by Apple. Nonetheless, it is essential to carefully review each duplicate set to confirm they are precise copies and not merely similar images.

CONCLUSIONS

FINAL THOUGHTS: EMBRACING TECHNOLOGY FOR A FULFILLING SENIOR LIFE

iPhone 15 can greatly enhance the lives of seniors, providing a pathway to a more fulfilling and connected existence. The iPhone 15 offers a multitude of features and applications that cater to the unique needs and interests of older individuals. From communication tools like video calls and messaging apps, seniors can effortlessly stay connected with loved ones, reducing feelings of isolation and loneliness. The iPhone 15 also grants access to a wealth of information at their fingertips, enabling seniors to pursue lifelong learning, explore new hobbies, and engage in mental stimulation. Health and fitness apps can assist in monitoring vital signs, tracking exercise routines, and managing medications, promoting overall well-being and independence. Additionally, the iPhone 15 offers entertainment options such as music streaming, e-books, and games, allowing seniors to relax and enjoy leisure activities. Embracing technology can empower seniors to lead vibrant, connected lives, fostering a sense of purpose and fulfillment, while breaking down barriers and expanding opportunities for engagement in the digital age.

CONTINUING YOUR LEARNING JOURNEY: STAYING UPDATED AND CONNECTED

The iPhone 15 provides a gateway to a vast array of knowledge and information, ensuring that you stay up-to-date with the latest news, trends, and developments in your areas of interest. With news apps and social media platforms readily available, you can effortlessly access news articles, blogs, and opinion pieces, enabling you to engage with current affairs and broaden your understanding of the world. Furthermore, the iPhone 15 allows you to connect with like-minded individuals through online communities, forums, and social networks, fostering meaningful connections and facilitating intellectual discussions. Whether it's joining virtual book clubs, participating in online courses, or attending webinars and conferences, the iPhone 15 opens doors to endless educational opportunities. Additionally, the iPhone's calendar and reminder features help you stay organized and manage your learning schedule effectively. Embracing the iPhone 15 as a tool for learning and connectivity empowers you to expand your horizons, cultivate new interests, and forge connections with a global community of learners, ultimately enriching your life and keeping your mind engaged.

❋ We Hope You're Loving Your Journey! ❋

Hello there, amazing reader! 😊

We're thrilled that you've embarked on this empowering journey with **"All-in-One iPhone 15 Guide for Seniors."**

We sincerely hope it's lighting up your path to mastering your **iPhone 15** and enriching your digital life. 🖩

If our guide has brought you closer to the tech-savvy, connected life you aspire to, we'd be over the moon if you could share your experience.

Your thoughts mean the world to us and **can help other seniors** <u>find their way to tech confidence and joy</u>, just like you did!

Could you take a moment to leave a positive review on Amazon.com? 📡

Your feedback not only warms our hearts but also supports us in reaching and helping more seniors embrace the digital age with ease and happiness.

☞ **Here's how you can spread the love:**

1. Visit Amazon.com.
2. Look up **"All-in-One iPhone 15 Guide for Seniors"**
3. Select 'Write a Customer Review.'
4. Express your insights, adventures, and beloved recipes!

Every word you share <u>helps build a community of tech-empowered seniors,</u> and **your support** is the beacon that guides them home.

Thank you for being a part of our journey.

Let's continue to explore, connect, and thrive together in this digital adventure. 🌐

With heartfelt gratitude,

Brandon Brooks and the "All-in-One iPhone 15 Guide for Seniors" Team